# Mountain Biking
# Southern
# New England

Paul Angiolillo

FALCON®
HELENA, MONTANA

# A FALCON GUIDE ®

Falcon® Publishing is continually expanding its list of recreational guidebooks. All books include detailed descriptions, accurate maps, and all information necessary for enjoyable trips. You can order extra copies of this book and get information and prices for other Falcon® books by writing Falcon, P.O. Box 1718, Helena, MT 59624 or calling toll free 1-800-582-2665. Also, please ask for a free copy of our current catalog. Visit our website at www.FalconOutdoors or contact us by e-mail at falcon@falconguide.com.

Library of Congress Cataloging-in-Publication Data

Angiolillo, Paul.
    Mountain biking southern New England / by Paul Angiolillo.
        p.     cm — (A Falcon guide)
    Rev. ed. of: The mountain biker's guide to sourthern New England. 1993
    Includes index
    ISBN 1-56044-748-6 (pbk.)
    1. All terrain cycling—New England—Guidebooks. 2. New England—Guidebooks.
I. Angiolillo, Paul. Mountain biker's guide to southern New England.   II. Title.
III. Series.
GV1045.5.N36A54 1999                                                  98-49647
917.404'43—dc21                                                          CIP

**CAUTION**

Outdoor recreational activities are by their very nature potentially hazardous. All participants in such activities must assume responsibility for their own actions and safety. The information contained in this guidebook cannot replace sound judgment and good decision-making skills, which help reduce risk exposure, nor does the scope of this book allow for disclosure of all the potential hazards and risks involved in such activities.

Learn as much as possible about the outdoor recreational activities in which you participate, prepare for the unexpected, and be cautious. The reward will be a safer and more enjoyable experience.

 Text pages printed on recycled paper.

# Table of Contents

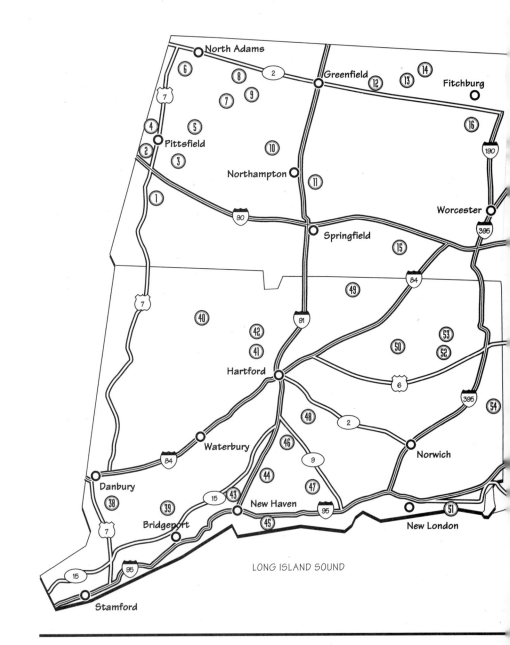

# MAP LEGEND

| | | | |
|---|---|---|---|
| Interstate | | Campground | |
| U.S. Highway | | Picnic Area | |
| State or Other Principal Road | | Buildings | |
| Forest Road | | Historical or Archeological Site | |
| Interstate Highway | | Peak/Elevation | 4,507 ft. |
| Paved Road | | Pass | |
| Unpaved/Gravel Road | | Bridge | |
| Unimproved Road or Double-track Trail | | Gate | |
| Trail (single-track) | | Parking Area | |
| Trailhead | | Railroad Track | |
| Waterway | | Cliffs/Bluff | |
| Lake/Reservoir | | Powerline/ Gas Line/ Cable Line | |
| Wetland/Swamp | | | |
| Falls | | Map Orientation | N |
| Forest Boundary | | Scale | 0   0.5   1  MILES |

# Acknowledgments

One of the pleasures of doing this book was meeting, talking with, and in several cases, riding with park supervisors and rangers. Almost without exception, these public officials took the time to review rides in this book. Some even volunteered to paint signs on trails, highlight maps, and show me around. Communicating with them made me—and I hope you—more confident about the openness of trails in public forests and parks in southern New England.

The names of these rangers appear below, along with the other people who helped to review rides and to create new ones, and otherwise made this book possible:

Alison Kozar Bamman, Sam Bartlett, Nadine Beckwith, Bill Boles, Peter Brandenberg, Bill Danielson, Gary Gilbert, Richard Haley, Rick Heath, Bob Hicks, John Keeney, Philip Keyes, Ron LeBlanc, Heather Linscott, Scott Menzel, Mitch McCulloch, John Pacheco, John Pelczarski, Dan O'Brien, Joe Ortoleva, Nancy Osher Blumberg, Jennifer Rummell, Richard Scott, Brian Smith, Alex Sokolow, Jim Thomas, Dee Todd, Dick Whiting, David Whitmon, and Mike Woyt.

Finally, for their patience and skill, I'd like to thank my editors at Falcon Publishing, John Burbidge and Larissa Berry.

Mountain biking can be an elevating activity. Pennwood State Park, Simsbury, Connecticut.

# What's Changed?

Put simply, this book has been completely revised, updated, and improved. Several rides that had become difficult or impossible to do (for various reasons) have been deleted, and they're replaced by 10 new rides. These new ones also fill some gaps in parts of the region. There are several more rides near Boston, a couple near New Haven, one more along the Connecticut coast, a new one in the Northampton/Amherst area, and a few more areas, including another ride in the Berkshires.

Just as important, I think, every ride in the book has been revised to make it both more complete and up-to-date. Many cyclists and park rangers (see Acknowledgments) helped to accomplish this job. And a set of greatly improved state trail maps for Massachusetts were invaluable in some cases.

Fortunately, there's almost all good news about changes to mountain biking in southern New England. Cyclists in the region have contributed to improving trails in dozens of areas, mainly through the New England Mountain Bike Association (NEMBA; see Information Sources on page 3 and the Appendix) and also through dialogues with rangers and other state officials to keep trails open. This is a lot more than just paying lip-service to trails—it's also down-to-earth work on weekend mornings (always followed by riding and socializing).

Through monetary grants, volunteers have rebuilt bridges, cut new trails, and, in one case, even saved an endangered turtle by rebuilding a fence around a wetlands. Furthermore, 14 NEMBA chapters have also sprung up throughout southern New England.

Overall, it's a healthier mountain biking scene in this region than it was five years ago—despite the rapid growth in the sport. And it's mainly due to the efforts of cyclists who love to ride in Massachusetts, Connecticut, and Rhode Island—in other words, people like you. To keep it that way, everyone should observe a few basic rules (see Trail Etiquette and Rules on page 2).

Finally, I'm sometimes asked: Do you have any extended, multi-day rides in your books? The answer is no—and yes. While the rides here are all doable in a day, many of them explore large areas with much more than a day's worth of riding opportunities. Many of them have camping sites, too. Also, the Ride Location Map in the front of the book shows, two or more rides are often within a short distance of each other. For instance, there are over a half-dozen rides in the scenic Berkshires in western Massachusetts within 10 to 20 miles of each other. Enjoy.

# Some Useful Information

The importance of riding on appropriate trails at a reasonable speed—and making sure others do the same—cannot be overemphasized. It takes just one or two inconsiderate cyclists to close a trail—or an entire park.

Observing these rules from the International Mountain Bicycling Association (IMBA)—and clueing in other riders to them—will go a long way toward keeping trails open for biking. You can contact IMBA at P.O. Box 7578, Boulder, CO 80306, (303) 545-9011, e-mail: imba@aol.com; www.imba.com.

### IMBA Rules of the Trail

The International Mountain Bicycling Association (IMBA) is a nonprofit advocacy organization dedicated to promoting mountain biking that's environmentally sound and socially responsible. IMBA's work keeps trails open and in good condition for everyone.

These rules of the trail are reprinted with permission from IMBA.

1. **Ride on open trails only.** Respect trail and road closures (ask if not sure), avoid possible trespass on land, obtain permits and authorization as may be required. Federal and state wilderness areas are closed to cycling. The way you ride will influence trail management decisions and policies.

2. **Leave no trace.** Be sensitive to the dirt beneath you. Even on open (legal) trails, avoid riding immediately after heavy rains or when the trail surface is soft and muddy. In some locations, muddy trails are unavoidable. Recognize different types of soils and trail construction. Practice low-impact cycling. This also means staying on existing trails and not creating new ones. Be sure to pack out at least as much as you pack in.

3. **Control your bicycle.** Inattention for even a second can cause problems. Obey all bicycle speed regulations and recommendations.

4. **Always yield trail.** Give your fellow trail users plenty of advance notice when you're approaching. A friendly greeting (or bell) is considerate and works well; don't startle others. Show your respect when passing by slowing to a walking pace or even stopping, particularly when you

meet horses. Anticipate other trail users around corners or in blind spots.

5. **Don't scare animals.** All animals are startled by an unannounced approach, a sudden movement, or a loud noise. This can be dangerous for you, others, and the animals. Give animals extra room and time to adjust to you. When passing horses use special care and follow the directions from the horseback riders; ask if uncertain. Running cattle and disturbing wildlife is a serious offense. Leave gates as you found them or as marked.

6. **Plan ahead.** Know your equipment, your ability, and the area in which you are riding, and prepare accordingly. Be self-sufficient at all times, keep your equipment in good repair, and carry all necessary supplies for changes in weather or other conditions. A well-executed trip is a satisfaction to you and not a burden or offense to others. Always wear a helmet.

## INFORMATION SOURCES

Please refer to "Appendix: Resources" for the contact addresses and phone numbers for the individual rides. It also includes the three key state agencies that dispense trail maps, camping brochures, and other information. Here are a few other ways to find out about mountain biking areas in southern New England.

The Internet is becoming the fastest way to find out about mountain biking sites. Since web sites can change, I haven't listed individual ones here. It's easy to use a web browser like Alta Vista, Yahoo, Lycos, or Excite. Just enter a few keywords—say, "mountain biking" and "Connecticut"—to locate all the sites about mountain biking in Connecticut. It's that simple.

The main mountain biking organization in this region is the New England Mountain Bike Association (NEMBA). Its web site, www.nemba.org, offers all kinds of information—including links to other web sites—about mountain biking in southern New England, including the local NEMBA chapters in the region. You can contact them at NEMBA, P.O. Box 2221, Acton MA 01720, 1-800-57-NEMBA, email: singletracks@nemba.org. If you live in the region, consider joining them.

Finally, local bike shops (often called "LBS" on Internet mailing lists and chat sites) are an excellent source of current information about rides, up-to-date trail conditions, access issues, and group rides. To find them, just use the Yellow Pages in a phone book (under "Bicycles") or a web site, such as www.Boston.com, and search under "Sports" and "Biking."

## PLAYING IT SAFE AND FUN

### Basic Equipment

Don't leave home without these items:

- A spare inner tube and patch kit
- Tire irons and Allen wrenches
- A portable air pump
- Plenty of water
- Some food
- A map

I also bring along other items to make a ride more enjoyable and safer—just as I would for a long hike:

- Compass
- Cyclocomputer (odometer)
- Few more repair tools, such as an adjustable wrench, spoke wrench, and small screwdriver
- Pencil wrapped in duct tape (two "tools" in one)
- Some bandages
- Bug repellent (depending on the season and terrain)
- Sunscreen
- Rain jacket and a spare pair of glasses (on longer rides)
- Wallet

Once while I was doing a group ride in a huge state forest, a dead branch jumped up and broke my derailleur. A guy came riding up behind me and pulled out a spare derailleur. Now *that's* preparedness.

### The Bike

You don't need an $800 rig to do a mountain bike ride, or even a $400 one. But you do need a bike that's in good condition. If you're doing a longer or more rugged ride on a new bike, be sure that it's had a check-up. There's nothing more frustrating than having a crank or headset come loose in the middle of a ride without the simple tool to fix it.

And, of course, if you're using a well-seasoned bike, be sure the tires are not too worn, the brake shoes aren't rubbing against the tires, the brake cables are in decent condition, and the chain is oiled.

### Maps

It's easy to forget that a map is not reality—it's a representation of reality. The latest computer-generated graphics can make a cool-looking map, but it's still just a symbol of the changing real world. In reality, developers build new roads—and obscure trailheads. Beavers dam streams. Ice storms fell trees. And sometimes, people cut new trails. The maps in this book are as accurate as possible, given the information at this time.

As I mention under some of the rides, though, a particular map might not show all the trails in an area, especially in the more elaborate trail networks. The alternative would have been to show only the trails on a single loop, with the cross-trails. Instead, I've tried to provide as many trails and roads for a ride as possible. Finally, I always bring along a compass.

### Seasons

Summer and fall are the best seasons for riding in southern New England. There's shade and less mud in the summer, and changing foliage and cooler weather in the fall. If there is little snow or ice, winter is also fine for riding (but be sure not to damage cross-country ski tracks). In many places in this region, riding in the off-season—between Labor Day and Memorial Day—can be quite enjoyable, since there's less traffic on the highways and trails.

Spring can be a more complicated season. Many trails are not in good shape for riding from around April through early June because of mud. If ridden, they can show deeper tires tracks, which can lead to complaints by other users. Dirt roads are usually less of a concern in the spring. Choose your ride accordingly—and stay flexible.

### Hunting Season

In the late fall and into the winter, hunting is allowed on some lands where you might be cycling. It's a good idea to check all signs at trailheads and parking lots to find out the local rules about this outdoor sport. Mountain biking is not usually a problem in southern New England during hunting season (unlike the deep woods in New Hampshire or Maine). But, it's always wise to wear colorful clothing; some cyclists also attach a bell to their bikes.

The dates for hunting season can vary from state to state, and it depends on the type of hunting—bow and arrow, rifle, bird, deer, etc. In Massachusetts, the major hunting season, mainly for deer, is from November 30 to December 20.

Hunting is not allowed on Sundays within 500 feet of a building, parking lot, picnic area, or campground, or within 150 feet of a paved road or bike path.

## HOW DIFFICULT IS A RIDE?

I should explain why this book doesn't provide a simple mileage and difficulty rating. Instead of documenting a single ride, I've tried to describe quite a few options at a site. Many of the rides give a suggested loop. By reading the few short paragraphs at the beginning of a ride and in "Notes on the trail," as well as referring to the map, you will be able to tell how difficult a ride will be.

## HOW TO USE THIS BOOK

Here's a brief description of each category in this book:

**General location:** Locates the ride in a town, and tells how far it is from nearby major roads and cities.

**Elevation change:** Tells how much climbing and descending there is on a ride, and whether the terrain is rolling or flat.

**Seasons:** Suggests the best seasons for riding at a site.

**Services:** Tells where to find water, restrooms, food, camping, bike shops, and other amenities. Note: Many state forests and parks in Massachusetts offer camping at inexpensive rates. The fees were not included in this book because they change every few years (depending on the governor). However, they're extremely reasonable ($4–$12 per night).

**Hazards:** Mentions aspects or sections of a ride that can be dangerous—like steep, difficult trails; sections used by equestrians; areas used during hunting season; or unmapped areas.

**Rescue index:** Gives the mileage for how far you will be from assistance.

**Land status:** Tells who owns the land.

**Maps:** Suggests where to find additional maps.

**Finding the trail:** Explains how to reach the trailhead (or trailheads) from major roads.

**Sources of additional information:** Gives the names of organizations for more information about a ride (with complete contact information in the Appendix: Resources).

**Notes on the trail:** Depending on the ride, describes either a particular loop, or gives several options for doing a ride.

# MASSACHUSETTS

# Western Massachusetts

## RIDE 1 *BEARTOWN STATE FOREST*

This moderately challenging 8-mile loop ride explores several long trails in an 11,000-acre forest in the heart of the Berkshires. The ride is actually made up of three interconnecting loops. First, you climb for a mile or so on a rugged double-track trail, with some mud in the flatter areas and loose rock and eroded areas on the steeper stretches. Then, you cruise along single-track trails for several miles, before descending on smoother dirt roads. In the winter, snowmobilers and cross-country skiers also use some of these trails.

Halfway along the ride, you reach a secluded pond. Nearby, along the trail, look for the stone walls and chimney of an old house. As you climb, watch how the woodscape changes from the darker, thicker, moister habitat of hardwood and softwood trees to a highland environment of smaller trees, bushes, and ferns.

Another popular ride in this large forest is a 12-mile or so loop that begins at the beach area of a 35-acre swimming pond at the forest's southern border. The map in this book shows only the northern part of this trail, once called the Bridle Trail.

The famous Appalachian Trail (known as the "AT") also runs through the forest—but it's off-limits for cycling. During the summer, this part of Massachusetts ("the Berkshires") attracts many visitors to its pastoral landscape and numerous cultural attractions, including the Tanglewood Music Festival and Jacob's Pillow Dance Theater.

**General location:** In the towns of South Lenox and Monterey, 4 miles south of Exit 2 on Interstate 90 (the Massachusetts Turnpike).

**Elevation change:** The ride climbs steadily and not too steeply for the first mile, then flattens and descends for a few miles, climbs again, and then descends for 2.5 miles. Total elevation gain is 400 feet.

**Seasons:** Any time between summer and late fall. The trails are rideable in the winter, too, if there has been little snowfall or if snowmobilers have packed them down. Expect mud in the spring.

**Services:** All services are available in Stockbridge and Lee to the north, and Great Barrington to the west. There is camping in the park (12 campsites, showers).

# RIDE 1 *BEARTOWN STATE FOREST*

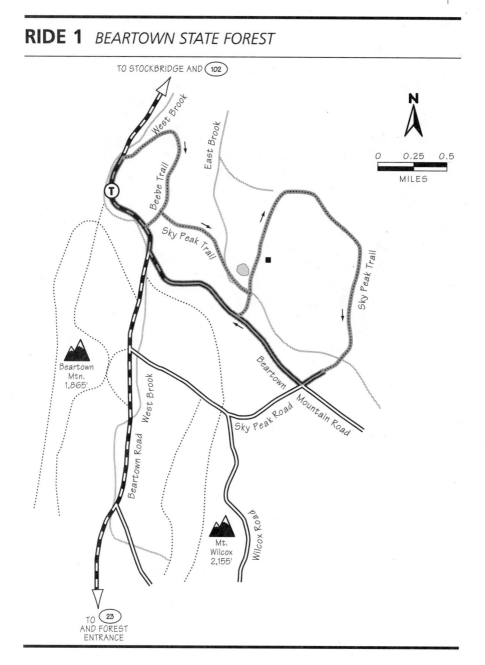

**Hazards:** At the beginning of the ride, the trail is somewhat eroded and can be wet. Also, watch out for occasional motorized off-road vehicles and light traffic on the steep paved descent on Beartown Road at the end of the ride.

A rugged double-track trail. Beartown State Forest, Monterey, Massachusetts.

**Rescue index:** At most you will be about 3 miles from assistance.

**Land status:** State forest trails and town roads.

**Maps:** Maps are available at kiosks at the beach area and parking lots, or from the Department of Environmental Management (see Appendix).

**Finding the trail:** Take Exit 2 off I-90 (the Massachusetts Turnpike), and head west on Massachusetts Highway 102 toward Stockbridge. After 3 miles, follow the brown forest signs to the left. After about 1.5 miles, you will pass a large brown forest sign on the right. Soon after the sign, just before a small bridge, park at turnoffs on the right or left.

**Sources of additional information:** Beartown State Forest (see Appendix).

**Notes on the trail:** Pick up the Beebe Trail on the eastern side of paved Beartown Road. (This is the wettest and most eroded part of the ride.) Climb steadily, veering to the right and following the yellow snowmobile signs. At the top of a climb, look for a single-track trail to the left. There may be a sign on a tree on the left, "Sky Peak Trail." (To do a short loop, just continue straight to reach unpaved Beartown Mountain Road.) After another mile or so, you will cross a small creek and soon afterward reach a dirt road at a secluded pond. Turn left, passing the pond (look for the stone walls and chimney of a former house on the right). Again, you can turn right on the dirt road and reach Beartown Mountain Road.

Just after passing the stone house, turn left to pick up the Sky Peak Trail again. (Despite its name, the Sky Peak Trail is a wooded ride.) A recent logging operation has cut another "road" straight ahead—be sure to turn left just after the pond to pick up the right trail.

After following the trail for several miles, curving to the right, you will come out on a wide dirt road (from another logging operation). Ride down this road to Beartown Mountain Road.

For a longer ride, continue across Beartown Mountain Road onto Sky Peak Road and then hook up with other unpaved roads and trails that eventually loop down to paved Beartown Road.

Otherwise, turn right on Beartown Mountain Road and descend to Beartown Road. Turn right again and descend to the trailhead.

# RIDE 2 *JOHN DRUMMOND KENNEDY PARK*

This moderate 6-mile loop ride runs through a handsome, compact park (known simply as "Kennedy Park") located just a few hundred feet from U.S. Highway 20 in Lenox. This quiet wooded area is full of scenic spots; large maple, birch, and black walnut trees; and the remnants of an old road and stone walls that led visitors to the Aspinwall Hotel, a private resort that once stood at the highest point.

As the official park map shows (see Maps on page 14), there are at least eight "points of interest" in the park, including a scenic overlook, a pond with benches, a large balancing rock, and a spring. At an overlook, you can see several mountain ranges, including Mt. Greylock to the north. The park is also popular among birders.

The 10 miles or so of trails here are blazed according to their difficulty (for cross-country skiing). You can climb gently on wide double-track trails or challenge yourself on tight, steep single-track. Main Trail is a wide, hard-packed woods road. At the other extreme, a rugged, grassy trail over a buried fiber-optic cable line also crosses the park.

Lenox, in the heart of the Berkshires, is a popular vacation town. In the summer, it comes alive with the Tanglewood Music Festival, which is the summer home of the Boston Symphony Orchestra; a world-famous dance performance shed, Jacob's Pillow Dance Theater; summer-stock theater; and film programs.

**General location:** The town of Lenox, just off US 20/US 7.

**Elevation change:** This terrain is rolling, with regular short climbs and descents.

# RIDE 2 *JOHN DRUMMOND KENNEDY PARK*

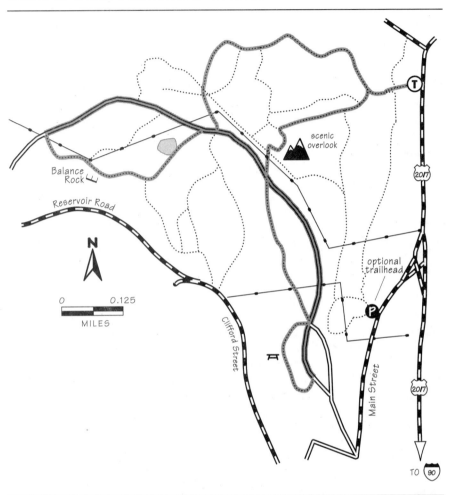

**Seasons:** Summer through late fall are best. Avoid wet trails in the spring and cross-country ski tracks in the winter.

**Services:** All services are available in Lenox and along US 20. There is a campground with showers at nearby October Mountain State Forest. To reach the campground, turn right in the center of Lee and follow the brown signs for the forest. The Arcadian Shop, a sports and bike shop at the trailhead in Lenox, sponsors group rides.

**Hazards:** None, except for some minor obstructions on the narrower trails.

Descending a single-track trail. John Drummond Kennedy Park, Lenox, Massachusetts.

Also, expect to meet other users, especially on weekends.

**Rescue index:** At most you will be about a half mile from a traveled road.

**Land status:** Town park trails. Local mountain bikers help to maintain the trails.

**Maps:** A trail map is available from the town of Lenox, or you can pick one up at the Arcadian Shop near the trailhead.

**Finding the trail:** Take Exit 2 off Interstate 90 (the Massachusetts Turnpike), onto US 20 West toward Lee and Lenox. The road divides into four lanes for a short distance in Lenox; just after it becomes two lanes again, you will pass a shopping center on the left. Immediately after the shops, turn left into the Arcadian Shop parking lot. The trailhead is at the far end of the parking lot, marked with a stonewall entrance.

**Sources of additional information:** Arcadian Shop or Lenox Town Hall (see Appendix).

**Notes on the trail:** You begin behind the Arcadian Shop. A double-track trail heads into the woods. At a four-way intersection just inside the forest there's a large trail map on a board. For a more challenging ride, follow a perimeter loop counterclockwise around the park. At the northwest border of the park, do not ride toward signs for the Audubon Sanctuary. Most trails are marked according to their level of difficulty.

# RIDE 3 *OCTOBER MOUNTAIN STATE FOREST*

This moderate 11-mile loop ride explores just a section of this largest state forest in Massachusetts (16,000 acres), using rugged jeep roads, smoother two-wheel-drive dirt roads, and a single-track trail.

This is grand and varied scenery, from highland woods, with giant pine trees sweeping the sky, to trail-hugging blackberry and red raspberry bushes that produce a sweet, natural snack in late August and early September. You will also pass two large lakes and a scenic overlook, and cross a dam.

For an easier ride, you can climb and descend the dirt roads that intersect in the forest. For more challenging riding, there's a network of single-track trails on the western side of the forest. The official trail map labels these trails as "shared use," which means that horses and motorized off-road vehicles also use them. Local mountain bikers ride on these trails, but some of them are hard to follow. *Note:* Rangers request that cyclists not use the hiking trails near the camping area or the trail around Felton Pond (on Schermerhorn Road).

The forest lies in the heart of Berkshire County, a popular vacation area in New England. Local towns such as Lenox and Becket boast many summer

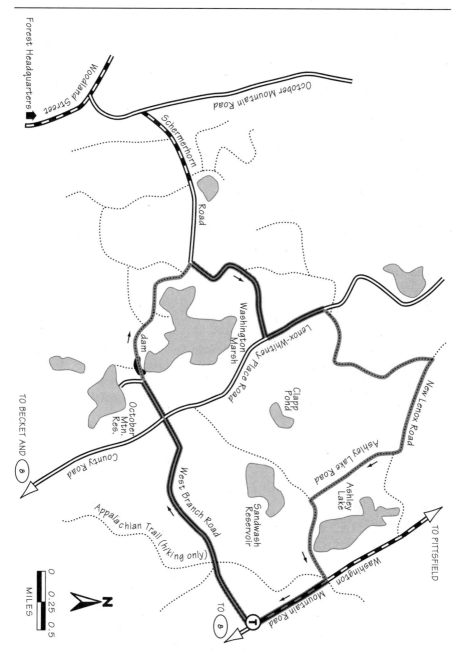

attractions, including the Tanglewood Music Festival, the summer residence of the Boston Symphony Orchestra; Jacob's Pillow, a world-class dance performance shed; live theater; and film programs.

**General location:** In the towns of Lenox, Washington, and Becket, 5 miles north of Interstate 90 (the Massachusetts Turnpike) and 6 miles south of Pittsfield.

**Elevation change:** The ride rolls gently up and down between about 1,700 feet and 1,900 feet.

**Seasons:** Summer through late fall is the best time, with plenty of colorful foliage in September and October.

**Services:** All services are available in Pittsfield, Lenox, and along U.S. Highway 20 and US 7. There's a campground in the forest (45 sites, with showers). To reach it, turn right in the center of Lee and follow the brown signs. The Arcadian Shop, a bike and sports store, is on US 20 in Lenox. It holds group rides.

**Hazards:** Watch for an occasional motorized vehicle on the two-wheel-drive roads.

**Rescue index:** At most, you will be about 2.5 miles from assistance on fairly secluded roads and trails.

**Land status:** State forest roads and trails.

**Maps:** Contact the Department of Environmental Management for a trail map (see Appendix). This agency provides maps of many state forests and parks in Massachusetts.

**Finding the trail:** You can reach the trailhead from either Pittsfield (to the north) or Becket (to the south). From the common in the center of Pittsfield, a lively hub city in western Massachusetts, turn east onto East Street, pass a large school, and fork right onto Elm Street. Blend left into Williams Street, and at Burgner Farm (a large farm stand with fresh foods and baked goods) fork right onto Washington Mountain Road. After 5 miles, turn right onto unpaved West Branch Road and park at a wide turnoff on the right (this is public land).

From the south, take Exit 2 on I-90 (the Massachusetts Turnpike) onto US 20 East toward Becket, and onto Washington Mountain Road heading north.

You can also begin riding farther inside the forest from the junction of West Branch and County roads. This junction can be reached from the south on County Road.

**Sources of additional information:** October Mountain State Forest (see Appendix).

**Notes on the trail:** Ride up four-wheel-drive West Branch Road until you reach an intersection with a huge clearing on the other side of it; helicopters sometimes land in this clearing. This is Four Corners. (You can also begin

A secluded woods road. October Mountain State Forest, Washington, Massachusetts.

riding here by driving north on County Road from Massachusetts Highway 8 in Becket.) Continue through the intersection, veering to the right on the road, and you will reach a large marsh, which was actually Washington Mountain Lake until 1992, and a dam. (The lake was drained in 1992 and will not be refilled.) Take the trail across the dam and pick up a double-track trail into the woods.

Follow this rocky trail in the woods, veering to the right, and you will come out on a dirt road, Schermerhorn Road. To take a side trip, turn left and reach a trail on the right heading toward Schermerhorn Gorge, a scenic landmark. Otherwise, turn right, climb past a scenic view on the left at the height-of-land, and reach a T junction with a four-wheel-drive dirt road, Lenox-Whitney Place Road. For an easier, shorter ride, turn right and return to Four Corners.

Otherwise, turn left onto Lenox-Whitney Place Road and, after less than a mile, turn right onto a narrower dirt road. Follow this eroded old road until it ends at the dirt New Lenox Road. Turn right, and after a mile, fork right onto the abandoned Ashley Lake Road. After about another mile, turn left onto another jeep road, passing attractive Ashley Lake on the left. You will come out on paved Washington Mountain Road, where the Appalachian Trail crosses it. (The AT is off-limits to cycling.) Turn right and ride back to West Branch Road.

# RIDE 4  *PITTSFIELD STATE FOREST*

At least 35 miles of trails and narrow roads connect up in this 9,695-acre forest. All of them are open to mountain bikers, except for a few hiking trails: the Pine Mountain, Parker Brook, Hawthorne, Tranquility, and Woods Ramble trails (see the Department of Environmental Management map available in the forest for the locations of all trails).

This elongated forest offers cyclists many different kinds of riding terrain— from shorter, easier single- and double-track trails fanning out from the main parking areas, to longer, steeper rides like the intermediate-level Balance Rock Loop Trail and the expert-level Honwee Loop Trail.

In particular, the trail around Balance Rock is a favorite among local cyclists, with its downhill stretch through a spruce forest. Balance Rock is a huge, 165-ton limestone boulder that was deposited on bedrock by retreating glaciers 12,000 years ago. Its base is only 3 feet wide.

Other sites in the forest include Berry Pond and Berry Mountain (more easily reached by hiking or by paved Berry Pond Circuit Road). At 2,150 feet, the pond is the highest natural body of water in Massachusetts. And the mountain comes alive with pink azaleas each June.

In the more secluded southern part of the forest (not shown on this map) the quasi-mystical Shaker communities once held music and dance sessions. Today, the 125-acre site is on the National Register of Historic Places. More old roads and trails interconnect in this area, sometimes challenging riders with their roughness and steepness. Try them out and you might do some shaking, too.

**General location:** Just west of Pittsfield and U.S. Highway 7.

**Elevation change:** The amount of climbing and descending will vary depending

# RIDE 4 *PITTSFIELD STATE FOREST*

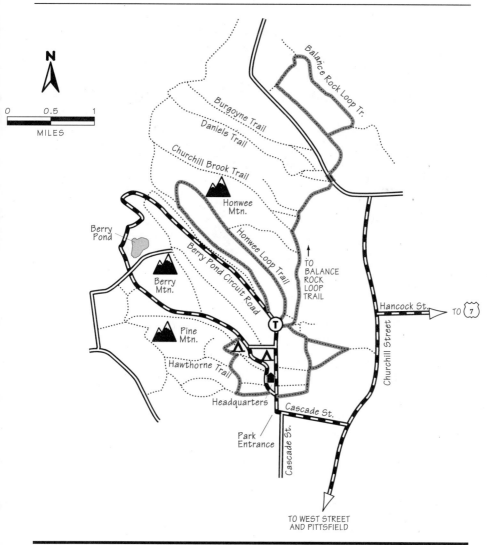

on the areas you ride in. The official forest trail map, available at the forest entrance and headquarters, has topographical lines on it. And see Notes on the trail on page 21 for more details about particular trails and loops.

**Seasons:** Summer and fall are best for riding.

**Services:** The forest has restrooms at the parking area, swimming at Lulu

A jeep road or a double-track trail—it's your choice. Pittsfield State Forest, Pittsfield, Massachusetts.

Brook, and two camping areas (31 sites, no showers). All other services are available in Pittsfield and on US 7 and US 20.

**Hazards:** Some loops, such as the Honwee Loop Trail, are rocky and difficult. Know your limits. Also, since this forest is quite large, be sure to allow plenty of time and carry plenty of water on longer rides. A compass will help you stay oriented.

**Rescue index:** At most you will be about 2 miles from assistance.

**Land status:** Multi-use roads and trails in a state forest.

**Maps:** A good trail map (with topographical contour lines on it) is available at the forest contact station (at the entrance) and headquarters.

**Finding the trail:** From the south on US 7, turn right onto West Street in downtown Pittsfield. After 2 miles, turn right onto Churchill Street, and after 1.8 miles, left onto Cascade Street. (Note: Ignore an earlier sign for "Cascade Street" on Churchill Street.) Follow the signs for the forest.

Inside the forest, to reach the main parking area, just go straight watching out for potholes. After passing the headquarters on the left and several trailheads, you will reach a large parking lot at a tree-shaded picnic area and a pond.

To reach a trailhead into the southern part of the forest, continue on West Street past Churchill Street. After another 1.5 miles, you will reach several parking lots at Berkshire Community College. Park in an open lot. Ride for

0.3 mile further on West Street, and you will reach the beginning of a dirt road into the forest.

From the north on US 7, turn right onto Hancock Road just after a large pond on the right. At the end of the road (1.8 miles), turn left onto Churchill Street. After 1 mile, turn right onto Cascade Street (across from a camp), and follow signs for the forest entrance.

**Sources of additional information:** Pittsfield State Forest (see Appendix).

**Notes on the trail:** As in many other larger state forests in Massachusetts, this one has a host of riding possibilities. You can do easier and shorter loops either east or west of the park entrance, access road, and headquarters. These are good "warm-up" areas—and a lot of fun. To the east, the double-track trails are flatter and fewer—and easier to follow. To the west, several of the single-track trails are reserved for hiking, but the rest are open for cycling. Don't ignore the small plastic blue arrows on trees, which can have the name of the trail written on them in casual black lettering. Also, look for posts in the ground with printed trail names on them at some junctions.

You pick up easier, shorter trails to the southeast just across the access road from the main parking area, at a jeep road heading downhill, just before the paved road veers toward the picnic area. After 0.1 mile, fork downhill to the right, and you will reach loops that turn southward and back toward the paved access road near the park entrance.

An excellent longer ride leaves the main parking area for the Balance Rock Loop Trail in the northern part of the forest. Begin at the same trailhead as the one for the loops to the southeast. This time, after 0.1 mile, fork left. You reach another fork: the left one connects to the difficult Honwee Loop Trail. The wider right-hand trail heads toward the Balance Rock Loop Trail, which is a gentler climb. (There should be trail signs at this junction.)

A steep, difficult ride on the Honewee Loop Trail also begins and ends at the main parking area, at steeper trailheads with signs.

You can also do shorter, fun single-track loops just west of the park entrance. *Note:* Several trails in this area are reserved for hiking: the Pine Mountain, Parker Brook, Hawthorne, Tranquility, and Woods Ramble trails; if you end up on one, it's easy to switch to an alternative. To reach this network of single-track trails, take a left turn on a paved road just after the forest entrance. Then, before reaching a parking lot, turn left onto a trail into the woods. Now it gets a bit confusing. Fork right, then left, and climb gently, reaching a small wooden bridge. At the three-way intersection, look for a sign marking the Hawthorne Trail. It will orient you. Cross the Hawthorne Trail and head northeast on a longer single-track trail, which eventually reaches paved Berry Pond Circuit Road. Then pick up another trail on the other side of the paved road, which will come out behind the main parking area.

The southern part of the forest, off West Street, has some relatively long, moderately difficult loops. To do a ride there, after entering the forest off West Street (see Finding the trail), take your first left turn onto the Civilian Conservation Corp Trail. Then you can take either the first or second right turn, and loop back using a section of the Taconic Skyline Trail (see map). Although its name is inviting, the Taconic Skyline Trail, which runs the entire length of the forest, is mostly muddy and eroded, since it's used by motorized off-road vehicles.

# RIDE 5 *WAHCONAH FALLS*

This "countryside cruise" makes a good afternoon or evening ride. It's an easy-to-moderate 5-mile loop that circumvents a small state park, first passing through an uninhabited woodscape, then the scenic countryside—using two-wheel-drive dirt roads, rugged double-track trails, and pavement.

After leaving the forest, you come out in the open countryside, eventually reaching a handsome horse farm, with wild raspberry bushes along the road.

A future mountain biker—and her chauffeur. Wahconah Falls State Park, Dalton, Massachusetts.

# RIDE 5  *WAHCONAH FALLS*

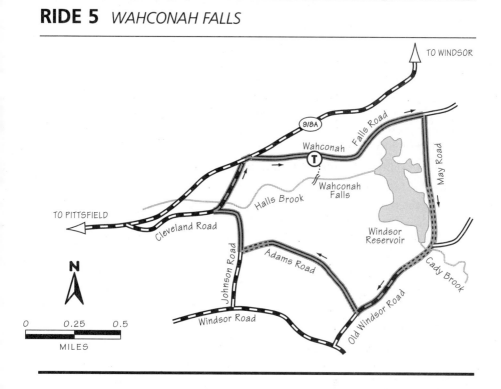

You'll get some exercise, too, since the beginning and end of the loop are climbs.

At the trailhead, there's a single-track trail across from the parking area and another dirt path leading down to the 40-foot falls, which spill into a swimming hole. It's a shady, invigorating spot—be sure to walk on the large, smooth rocks at the base of the falls, or just sit and take in the waterfall.

Nearby Pittsfield is a lively hub in western Massachusetts, with many cultural and social offerings.

**General location:** Just off Massachusetts Highway 9/8A, between Dalton and Windsor, 8 miles east of Pittsfield.

**Elevation change:** The ride begins with a short, somewhat steep climb. It then descends and rolls, before climbing back to the parking lot.

**Seasons:** This can be a four-season ride. Expect muddy roads in the spring.

**Services:** All services are available along MA 9 and in Dalton and Pittsfield.

**Hazards:** None, except for the occasional rugged stretch on the jeep trails. And watch out for the occasional vehicle on the two-wheel-drive roads.

**Rescue index:** At most you will be about a half mile from assistance.

**Land status:** Town and state park roads.

**Maps:** A detailed road map will show these roads.

**Finding the trail:** On MA 9/MA 8A, between Dalton and Windsor, watch for brown signs for the state park. Turn onto North Street (from the east it's a left turn about 3.5 miles west of the junction of MA 9 and MA 8A). Then fork right onto hard-packed dirt Wahconah Falls Road, and you'll reach a large parking area on the right. If the lot is gated, just park along the road in front of it. As always, lock your vehicle.

**Sources of additional information:** Wahconah Falls State Park, c/o Pittsfield State Forest (see Appendix).

**Notes on the trail:** This clockwise ride is easy to follow: Just turn right at all major intersections. First climb the road through the park, passing a couple of beckoning side roads. Turn right at a three-way junction. After about a half mile, this road (May Road) ends at a "Closed" sign—but the double-track trail ahead is open. Continue onto the trail and come out on a two-wheel-drive road (near a home). Veer right, cross a bridge, veer right again, and reach a paved road. Turn right on it, and after less than a half mile, turn right again onto narrower, unpaved Adams Road. This road becomes a jeep trail, crosses a powerline (which appears to be rideable to the left), and reaches a two-wheel-drive road (Johnson Road). Turn right on it, and you will come out at a paved road across from a horse farm (Cleveland Road). Turn right and reach MA 9. Turn right, ride on the wide shoulder for 100 feet, veer right onto Wahconah Falls Road, and climb back to the parking lot—and the cooling falls.

# RIDE 6 *MOUNT GREYLOCK STATE RESERVATION*

This oldest state forest in Massachusetts has reserved several old roads and trails for mountain biking, and there's a climb on a secluded dirt road to a scenic overlook. Plan to visit this huge reservation (12,000 acres) for a complete outdoor experience: camping sites in the woods; hiking trails and loops such as the Appalachian Trail; various ways to reach the highest peak in the state, Mt. Greylock (3,491 feet); and mountain biking. A road-bike race to the top of Mt. Greylock on ultra-steep, paved Notch and Rockwell roads is held annually.

This chapter highlights two out-and-back rides (or one-way to a pick-up spot). The more rugged ride climbs and descends for about 4.5 miles through deep woods from a trailhead on Rockwell Road to a parking area at the end of

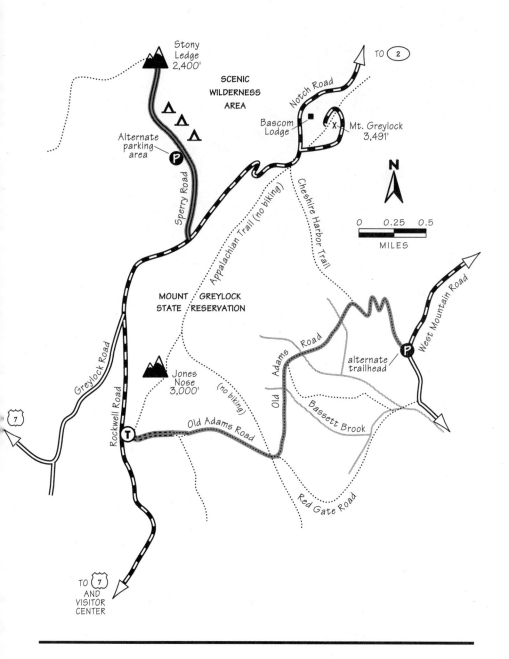

Panoramic view of a wilderness area. Mount Greylock State Reservation, Adams, Massachusetts.

the Cheshire Harbor Trail (which is entirely open for biking)—with an optional, more difficult loop possible (Red Gate Road). Along the way, you will cruise on a shady single-track trail past a dramatic tree-lined gorge (Old Adams Road).

A separate 3-mile (round-trip) out-and-back ride reaches a panoramic overlook using a scenic dirt road (Sperry Road) that climbs past the camping sites. Stony Ledge Trail descends from the overlook at the top of Sperry Road. A former downhill ski trail, it's now a designated mountain bike trail—but it's treacherous when wet, which is most of the time. Ride it at your own risk.

The Appalachian Mountain Club (AMC) lodge at the summit of Mt. Greylock has overnight accommodations and sponsors many events in the summer, including lectures, guided tours, and cultural events. For less-strenuous exercise, check out pastoral Williams College and the world-class Clark Art Institute in nearby Williamstown.

**General location:** In the northwest corner of Massachusetts, just south of North Adams, Williamstown, and Massachusetts Highway 2.

**Elevation change:** On Old Adams Road, you'll roll up and down, with several moderate climbs along the way. The Cheshire Harbor Trail is steeper; refer to the official trail map, available at various sites in the reservation. And it's a steady, not-too-steep climb on smooth dirt to Stony Ledge for a mile.

**Seasons:** Summer and fall are best. Expect plenty of mud in the spring.

**Services:** All services are available on U.S. Highway 7, MA 2, and in Lanesboro, North Adams, and Williamstown, including two mountain bike shops in Williamstown—the Mountain Goat on Water Street and The Spoke on Main Street. There is camping on the reservation.

**Hazards:** Watch for eroded downhill sections on Old Adams Road. Remember that mossy, green areas on exposed rock are slippery. On Sperry Road, stay to the right and be aware of other vehicles.

**Rescue index:** At most you will be about 2 miles from help on secluded old roads.

**Land status:** Old roads in a state reservation.

**Maps:** Trail maps are stocked at various sites in the reservation, including at the contact station on Sperry Road and the visitor center (see Appendix).

**Finding the trail:** You can reach the trailhead—called Jones Nose after a nearby landmark—from US 7 or MA 2. The easiest route is from US 7 (Main Street) south of the reservation in Lanesboro. Take North Main Street and follow signs for the forest. Fork left at the visitor center and continue for 3.5 miles on paved Rockwell Road, turning right into a large, unpaved parking area (where a hiking trail goes to Jones Nose).

You can also take a secluded, narrow two-wheel-drive dirt road, Greylock Road, from US 7 to the trailhead. Greylock Road is 8 miles south of Williamstown, and winds and climbs for about 3.5 miles to Rockwell Road. Then turn right and look for the trailhead, Jones Nose, on the left.

For a scenic, *steep* route from the north, you can turn off MA 2 in North Adams onto Notch Road, and climb on pavement for several miles over the top of Mount Greylock—this is a major ascent and descent. You will come down the other side on Rockwell Road and turn left into the Jones Nose parking area.

**Sources of additional information:** Mount Greylock State Reservation (see Appendix) or two bike shops in Williamstown, the Mountain Goat and The Spoke.

**Notes on the trail:** From the Jones Nose parking area, ride around the gate and downhill on Old Adams Road. After a half mile, just before crossing a small brook, fork left, staying on Old Adams Road. (The right trail is a scenic single-track trail that heads toward the town of Cheshire. After about a mile, you can fork off this trail and eventually reach West Road and West Mountain Road— but it's wiser to do this loop with a local rider.)

After this first turn on Old Adams Road, you climb steadily and gently for almost a mile. At this point, you can take another trail, Red Gate Road, sharply to the right. It will eventually loop around to West Mountain Road. But it's quite eroded in places. On it, you will descend, parallel and cross a brook, climb again, come out on a wider trail, turn left, climb, veer right, and finally come out at the trailhead at West Mountain Road. From there, you can climb on the Cheshire Harbor Trail to Old Adams Road.

Otherwise, stay on Old Adams Road for about 2 miles, until you reach the Cheshire Harbor Trail. Now you can go downhill on several switchbacks for about a mile to reach a parking area at West Mountain Road.

For an out-and-back ride to a spectacular view: from a parking area on dirt Sperry Road, climb on this two-wheel-drive road for about 1.5 miles, reaching a picnic area at a scenic overlook, Stony Ledge.

# RIDE 7 *WINDSOR STATE FOREST*

Beginning at a swimming beach on a sparkling river, this 10-mile loop ride winds underneath a cathedral-like canopy of trees, passes a scenic falls, rolls through open countryside, passes an abandoned farm and a nineteenth-century cemetery—and that's just on the first half.

The terrain on this ride alternates between 6 miles of narrow, scenic two-wheel-drive dirt roads and 4 miles of rugged jeep trails. At the end of the ride, there's an optional half mile on a single-track trail.

Less than a mile from the trailhead, you will pass one of the forest's main attractions, Windsor Jambs, a series of scenic falls tumbling over water-smoothed bedrock in a shady gorge. Halfway into the ride (on Upper Road), look for vistas through the treeline, as well as wild red raspberry bushes, which ripen in July.

For more relaxation, you can also swim, picnic, and/or camp in the forest. (There's a modest fee to park and swim.)

**General location:** Town of Windsor, 3 miles north of Massachusetts Highway 9, and about 8 miles south of MA 8A.

**Elevation change:** You will begin riding at 1,350 feet and reach 1,850 feet after 7 miles.

**Seasons:** This can be a four-season ride, with the usual pockets of mud in the spring and wetter weather.

**Services:** There are water and restrooms at the headquarters. All other services are found along MA 9. The forest has 25 campsites.

**Hazards:** Be prepared to switch riding techniques from the two-wheel-drive roads to narrower, rougher roads and trails.

# RIDE 7  *WINDSOR STATE FOREST*

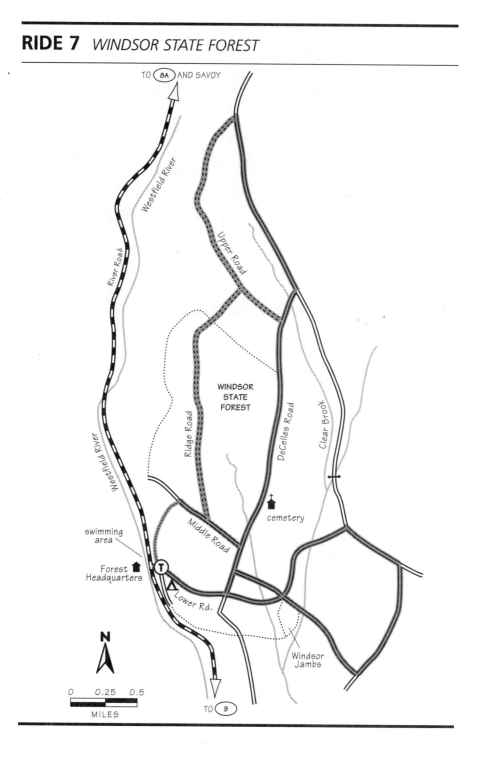

TO (8A) AND SAVOY

Westfield River

River Road

Upper Road

WINDSOR
STATE
FOREST

Ridge Road

DeCelles Road

Clear Brook

Westfield River

cemetery

Middle Road

swimming
area

Forest
Headquarters

Lower Rd.

Windsor
Jambs

N

0    0.25    0.5
MILES

TO (9)

A relaxation spot. Windsor State Forest, Windsor, Massachusetts.

**Rescue index:** At most you will be about 2 miles from assistance on easily traversed old roads.

**Land status:** Roads and trails on public land and town roads.

**Maps:** Maps are available at the trailhead or from the Department of Environmental Management (see Appendix).

**Finding the trail:** From the south, on MA 9, about 6 miles east of Windsor, watch for the brown sign for the state forest—it's a sharp turn on a hill. From the east, it's a left turn at the road for "West Cummington and Windsor Jamb." Follow the signs for the forest; after 3 miles, you will pass campsites and reach the parking lot at the forest headquarters and swimming beach.

From the north, you can reach the parking area from MA 8A, by turning southward on River Road in Savoy. There's no sign for the forest on River Road, though, which is 4.5 miles west of the junction of MA 8A and MA 116.

**Sources of additional information:** Windsor State Forest (see Appendix).

**Notes on the trail:** This ride explores many of the trails and roads in this forest by joining together five smaller loops. You can do them as shorter rides, too. First, head across the wide stream away from the parking area and begin climbing on gravel Lower Road. After less than a half mile, you will cross an intersection. This is where the ride will come out on the left. Continue straight to another intersection. Turn right and you will pass the scenic falls, Windsor Jambs, on the right.

Then the road leaves the state forest, becoming a more rugged trail and going steadily downhill. It comes out on a two-wheel-drive dirt road. Turn left, veer left again, and you will reach a three-way intersection with a sign indicating a left turn toward the state forest.

Turn left (the road on the right is a dead-end), and you will re-enter the intersection that you passed on the way to Windsor Jambs. For a shorter ride, continue straight to return to the trailhead. Otherwise, turn right at the intersection, climb on a four-wheel-drive road, and you will reach a T junction, with an abandoned farm and campsite on the other side. Turn right and pass an old cemetery on the right.

Continue climbing and watch for scenic views between the trees on the right. Then, while descending, watch for a left turn onto a rugged jeep trail (Upper Road). Turn left on it and climb gently for almost a mile. You will come out on a two-wheel-drive dirt road. You can shorten the entire ride by turning left on this road. Otherwise, turn right, fork right after less than a mile, then fork right again. You are back on the road that passed the cemetery (it's called both Decelles Road and Windago Road).

Turn onto Upper Road again (this time it comes up on the right), and now take the first sharp left turn onto a grassy road (Ridge Road). At a field, you will reach a T junction with Middle Road.

Now you can turn left, reaching Decelles Road again, turn right, reach Lower Road, and turn right toward the trailhead. For a single-track ride, turn right onto Middle Road, and watch for a trail on the left marked with blue blazes. This overgrown single-track trail comes out behind the camping area near the trailhead.

---

# RIDE 8 *SAVOY MOUNTAIN STATE FOREST*

This huge, high-altitude forest (11,000 acres at around 2,000 feet) has enough smooth, narrow, secluded dirt roads and multi-use trails (about 20 miles of trails) for several days of mountain biking. For the complete outdoor experience, you can also swim, camp, or picnic around its ponds, as well as visit several scenic areas in the forest by bike.

Notes on the trail on page 33 offers two suggestions for loops, using both trails and roads, which you can combine or modify. Remember they're merely recommendations. Don't feel shy about asking local riders and rangers about other possibilities—virtually all the trails and roads in this well-maintained forest are open for mountain biking.

Because of its altitude, this forest is similar to woodlands in Vermont, with balsam, fir, hemlock, red spruce, and many other varieties of trees and shrubs.

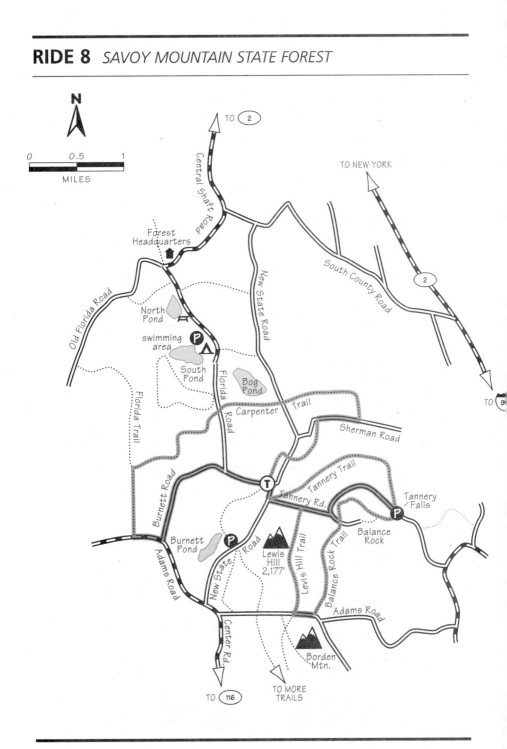

There's also excellent fishing (trout, bass, and perch) at Bog Pond, as well as other denizens of the forest, including beaver, porcupines, and birds.

If you're looking for Savoy Mountain itself, its name was changed to Borden Mountain sometime in the past. Colonial settlers came to this area to log and farm. You can find remnants of their industry in the forest, in the form of cellar holes, stone walls, graveyards, and sawmill sites.

For a bit of culture or intellectual stimulation, visit nearby Williamstown, the home of Williams College and the Clark Art Institute, renowned for its collections of Impressionist and American paintings.

**General location:** Town of Florida, 4 miles south of Massachusetts Highway 2.

**Elevation change:** There can be quite a bit of climbing and descending in this forest on both the roads and trails—or less if you choose some loops. The official trail map—available at several sites throughout the forest, including the parking areas and ponds near the main entrance—has topographical contour lines.

**Seasons:** Any time between late spring and late fall is good.

**Services:** The forest offers swimming and camping (45 campsites) from mid-May to mid-October, restrooms, and water. All other services are available in Savoy and along MA 2 to the north and MA 116 to the south.

**Hazards:** Some of the trails are eroded—know your limits. On the dirt roads, keep an ear out for the occasional motorized vehicle.

**Rescue index:** At most you will be about 1.5 miles from assistance.

**Land status:** State forest roads and trails.

**Maps:** A good forest trail map with contour lines is available at various places in the forest, including the headquarters.

**Finding the trail:** From MA 2 in the town of Florida, watch for a brown state forest sign (on the right from the east), and turn south on Central Shaft Road. After 3.5 miles, following signs for the forest, you will reach the state forest. Continue on unpaved Florida Road, watching out for potholes. Turn left onto Burnett Road and 6 miles from MA 2, just before the dirt road veers left, turn left into a large gravel parking area. There are also several other parking areas in the forest (see map).

From the east on MA 2, you can take a shortcut on more rugged South Country Road, which is a left turn 2 miles after the "Entering Florida" sign.

From the south, turn north off MA 116 in Savoy (just east of a fire station) onto Center Road. After climbing for a couple of miles, the road veers sharply left and soon turns right onto patchy New State Road. After 1.3 miles, turn left onto dirt Florida Road and immediately right into the parking area.

**Sources of additional information:** Savoy Mountain State Forest (see Appendix).

**Notes on the trail:** Here are two possible loops. Many key junctions and trailheads in the forest are marked with signs. Loop 1: Turn left out of the

A friendly sign at a trailhead. Savoy Mountain State Forest, Savoy, Massachusetts.

parking lot and fork right immediately onto New State Road. Cross a small bridge, and after just 0.2 mile, turn left onto narrow Tannery Road. After climbing, you can turn right (southward) off this jeep road onto the Lewis Hill Trail, reach Adams Road, turn left on it, and left again (northward) onto Balance Rock Trail. After visiting Balance Rock on a side trail, take Tannery Road again, turn right, and, before reaching another parking area, turn left sharply onto Tannery Trail, which heads back toward the trailhead.

Loop 2: Take the rugged multi-use trail on the northern side of the parking area, cross New State Road, and continue on this rugged trail until it intersects Sherman Road. Then turn left onto the Carpenter Trail. Now you can loop back on smoother New State Road or continue on Carpenter Trail as it crosses the forest, hooks up with the Florida Trail, and veers south to Adams Road; go left along the road and left (northward) on Burnett Road, which takes you back to Florida Road and the trailhead.

# RIDE 9 *HAWLEY*

This moderate ride through both woods and open countryside combines an 8.5-mile loop and a 4-mile loop. Using secluded two-wheel-drive roads, the longer loop explores a forest of pine, birch, maple, hemlock, ash, and oak trees; and passes stone walls, a wetland, fields, a nineteenth-century cemetery, the village of Hawley, and a defunct 30-foot-high brick-making kiln—which you can explore.

Next, you leave Kenneth Dubuque Memorial State Forest (known familiarly as "Hawley" forest), pass a local swimming pond, and take a secluded four-wheel-drive road past a historical house (1789) and an abandoned farm site with an old apple orchard, blueberry bushes, and a view of a nearby mountain.

At the trailhead, there's a short single-track trail to the remains of an old mill, built over a river. It was once the site of a large tannery, which kept many local citizens employed.

This ride can be easily extended into two adjoining state forests—Savoy Mountain and Mohawk—or a weekend or several days of riding.

**General location:** On Massachusetts Highway 8A, just south of West Hawley and a few miles south of MA 2 (the Mohawk Trail). Most of the ride is in Kenneth Dubuque Memorial State Forest.

**Elevation change:** At the beginning of the ride, you climb steadily from 1,500 to 1,800 feet. Then it's downhill and rolling for the rest of the ride.

**Seasons:** This can be a four-season ride (with the usual muddier conditions in the spring).

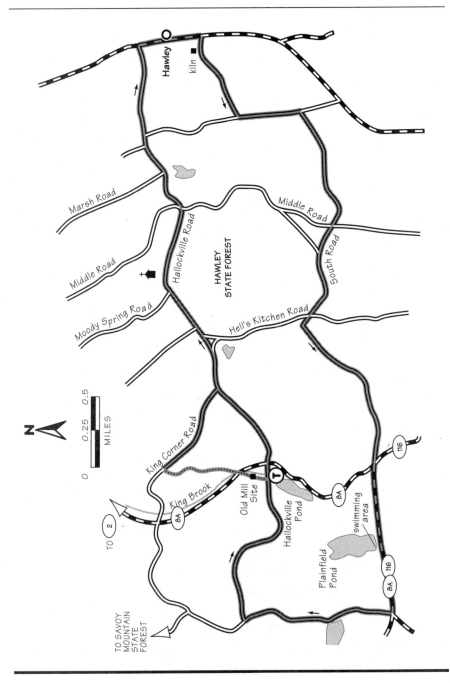

**Services:** All services are available in Dalton (southwest) and North Adams (northwest).

**Hazards:** Watch out for occasional vehicles on the two-wheel-drive and paved roads. Also, remember that these are deep woods; it's easy to take a wrong turn and become temporarily disoriented. A compass and regular checking of the map will help.

**Rescue index:** At most you will be about 2 miles from assistance on secluded roads.

**Land status:** Old town roads and public trails, most of them in a state forest.

**Maps:** USGS, 7.5-minute series, Plainfield, Mass.

**Finding the trail:** From the south on MA 8A, watch for a large gate at a pond on the left, 1 mile north of the junction of MA 8A and MA 116. If the gate is closed, park along the road near the gate but not blocking it.

From the north on MA 2, turn south onto MA 8A in Charlemont. After 8 miles, you will pass the parking area on the right.

**Sources of additional information:** Department of Environmental Management (see Appendix).

**Notes on the trail:** The turns and junctions on this ride are distinct—but there are quite a few of them, and it can be easy to take the wrong fork while cruising along. Refer to the map, and a compass might also help you stay oriented.

You can begin either on a woods road or a more challenging single-track trail past the historic mill site. To take the road, head north on paved MA 8A from the trailhead for a few hundred yards and turn right on a woods road (Hallockville Road). To begin the ride on the trail, cross a dirt road next to the pond, and take a single-track trail marked "Mill Site Trail." This is a hiking trail that requires carrying your bike across a few stretches. You will see the old mill in the river (on the right). Keep veering right and you will soon reach paved MA 8A. Just across the highway, an overgrown opening with several wide birch log steps leads into the woods, at a sign reading "Hawley Path Trail." Take this trail and almost immediately turn left in the woods, paralleling the highway.

After 1 mile on this lightly maintained trail, you will come out at a T junction on a narrow dirt road (King Corner Road). Turn right, uphill, and you will soon reach another T junction with a wider dirt road (Hallockville Road). This is the road you can take directly from the trailhead.

Turn left on this road, reach a pond on the right, and then fork left. (It's easy to unintentionally fork right here onto Hell's Kitchen Road.) Next, you will pass Moody Spring Road on the left, which heads north toward a spring. Then you will pass a field and shelter recessed on the right and a well-maintained old cemetery.

Checking out the remnants of a large kiln. Hawley, Massachusetts.

At the next junction, turn left, and almost immediately right at a fork and cross a small brook. (You can turn right at the first junction to do a shorter loop.) After climbing some more and passing another crossroad, you will go through a brown gate, leaving the state forest. Reaching pavement, turn right and ride through the village of Hawley. You will pass a fire station on the right; immediately after it turn right into a parking area and onto a dirt road heading back into the forest.

After a short distance, you can fork right into a clearing to visit the abandoned kiln. Then continue in to the left (west), descending a steep hill. You will reach a T junction with a stone wall. Turn left on a more rugged road, then right at the next junction, onto South Road. This becomes a two-wheel-drive dirt road and comes out on MA 116. Turn right and you will reach the intersection of MA 116 and MA 8A.

To do a 4-mile loop, go straight on MA 116 North/MA 8A South. (Otherwise, turn right onto MA 8A north and ride for 1 mile back to the trailhead.) After a half mile on MA 116 north, you will pass a public beach on Plainfield Pond on the right. After another half mile, turn right onto a hard-packed dirt road heading uphill. You will pass another pond on the left, Crooked Pond, and a few homes, including a house built in 1789. After a couple of miles, you arrive in a clearing with an abandoned orchard and a view of Borden Mountain ahead. Once past the clearing, veer right, staying on the main road, and you will reach the trailhead on MA 8A.

# RIDE 10 *D.A.R. STATE FOREST*

This moderately challenging 5-mile ride circumvents a 1,500-acre forest that's full of scenic areas—dramatic woodscapes, two lakes, and a lookout—and 10 to 15 miles of trails and dirt roads. This ride uses mainly single-track trails, some of them rugged and steep in places. Less-experienced riders can walk through the more difficult sections or stay mainly on the woods roads.

The scenic highlight is a panoramic view of the foothills of the Berkshire Mountains from a fire tower, which you can reach by either a dirt road or a trail. Along the ride, you will also pass tall evergreen and deciduous trees; midlevel mountain laurel bushes, which flower in June and July; blueberry bushes, ripening in late summer; and low-lying ferns and witch hazel plants.

This 1,600-acre state forest (D.A.R. stands for Daughters of the American Revolution) is also a popular swimming and camping spot, with 50 campsites, including hot showers.

There's a nearby scenic area on the Westfield River on Massachusetts Highway 9, 3.5 miles west of its junction with MA 112.

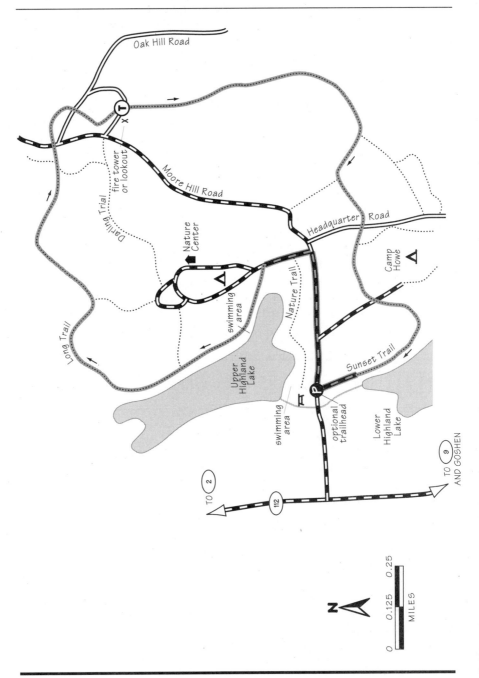

**General location:** The town of Goshen, off MA 112, 15 miles northwest of Northampton.

**Elevation change:** The ride begins by descending for 250 feet, then climbs steadily for 300 feet, and descends 50 feet to the trailhead.

**Seasons:** Late spring through late fall is good for riding here. Expect some wetness in the spring.

**Services:** Water, restrooms, and camping are available in the forest. All other services are in Goshen and Northampton.

**Hazards:** Several stretches of trail are steep and obstructed—know your limits. (A tip: Lower your saddle before descending on steeper terrain.) You might encounter horseback riders and hikers on the trails; be considerate of these slower-moving users.

**Rescue index:** At most, you will be about 1 mile from assistance.

**Land status:** Trails and roads on public land.

**Maps:** USGS, 7.5-minute series, Goshen, Mass.

**Finding the trail:** On MA 112, just north of Goshen, look for brown signs for the state forest, which is on your right from the south. There is a modest fee to park and swim at the beach. Pass the toll booth and swimming beach, and climb on paved Moore Hill Road through the forest for about 1.25 miles. Just beyond the height-of-land, turn right onto a dirt road marked "Fire Tower." After 0.3 mile, you will reach a grassy turnoff on the right.

**Sources of additional information:** D.A.R. State Forest (see Appendix).

**Notes on the trail:** Here's a detailed description of one loop. (You can also begin riding nearer the forest entrance; see map). Across from the parking area, ride through the gate and immediately turn left onto a single-track trail heading south into the woods. Follow the red diamond arrows on the trees. (Sometimes you must look for pieces of a marker nailed to a tree rather than an entire arrow, if the marker has been broken.) After the trail descends steeply, it reaches a flat area and veers to the right, crosses a brook, and climbs gently. Still rising slightly, it turns right again, crosses another small brook, and meets a trail marked with yellow blazes. Stay with the red blazes. You will reach an intersection in the woods with arrows on several trees. Turn left, following the smaller red arrows with horses on them. You will reach a woods road, Headquarter Road. (For a shorter loop, you can turn right and return to Moore Hill Road.)

Then turn right on the dirt road, and almost immediately pick up the trail on the other side, now marked with a blue maple leaf. After about a half mile, you will cross a paved road leading into Camp Howe. (There is a row of water spigots at a large basin just inside the camp.) Pick up the trail on the other side of the road and you will soon reach Lower Highland Lake.

Veer right along the lake and you will come out at a paved boat-launching site. Turn right on the pavement (watching out for walkers and other users).

A fern-swept trail. D.A.R. State Forest, Goshen, Massachusetts.

Ride along this paved road for about a half mile, and turn left at signs for campsites and a boat ramp. Ride a short distance past the boat launching area on the left, and then fork left at a sign for the trail.

Follow the blue trail markers across a dirt road and along the lake (Upper Highland Lake). You will pass the sign "Long Trail to fire tower, 2.3 miles." This is the trail you want. At the northern end of the lake, it veers into the woods, following blue markers (or the remains of them). After about 2 miles, fork to the left, following more signs for the fire tower. Soon you will come out at paved Moore Hill Road. You can take the trail just across the road or the dirt road to the right of it, to reach the fire tower. Use a dirt access road heading south from the tower to return to the parking area.

# Central Massachusetts

## RIDE 11 HOLYOKE RANGE STATE PARK

This convenient, yet secluded forest offers at least 10 miles of trails—all open for mountain biking, except for a few trails near the busier Visitor Center. The park has a variety of riding conditions, from smoother woods roads and flatter paths to rock-strewn jeep roads and more difficult single-track trails. Although the 3,000-acre park is surrounded by a landscape of orchards, farmland, and five colleges, you feel like you're in a more rugged place, like New Hampshire, with trails winding through deep woods.

In fact, this range is unique in the region because it runs east-west, instead of the usual north-south. This makes its habitat both northern and southern. The southern portion of the park is dominated by American beech, sugar maple, and various nut trees, like ash and hickory. The northern part is populated by white, red, black, and chestnut oaks, along with beech and birch trees. The ravines in between contain white pine and eastern hemlock trees, giving cyclists deep, dark, cool places to cruise.

While you're riding, also keep an eye out for the abundant wildlife. White-tailed deer, porcupines, and various squirrels live in these food-rich oak forests. Birds abound—wild turkey, ruffed grouse, barred and great horned owls, and a plethora of songbirds.

Nearby, one can visit lively campuses in this famous five-college area: Hampshire College, Amherst College, and the University of Massachusetts in Amherst; Mount Holyoke College in South Hadley; and Smith College in Northampton.

**General location:** Town of Amherst, about 6 miles east of Interstate 91, 10 miles east of Northampton, and 95 miles west of Boston.

**Elevation change:** Rolling terrain, with regular short, sometimes steep, climbs and descents, and no large hills. From either the north or south, it's generally climbing for a while, then rolling, and downhill.

**Seasons:** Summer and fall are best for riding here. Expect some blowdowns across the trails in the spring.

**Services:** Water and restrooms are available at the Notch Visitor Center on Massachusetts Highway 116. All other services are available along MA 116, in

# RIDE 11  *HOLYOKE RANGE STATE PARK*

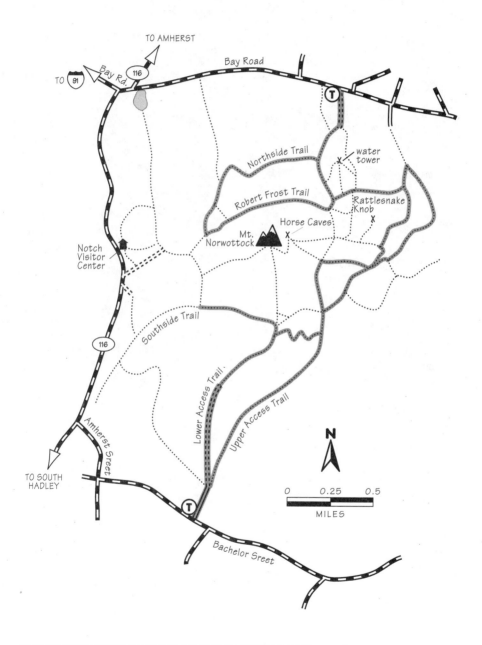

TO AMHERST

Bay Road

Bay Rd.

TO 91

116

Northside Trail

water tower

Robert Frost Trail

Rattlesnake Knob

Horse Caves

Mt. Norwottock

Notch Visitor Center

Southside Trail

116

Lower Access Trail

Upper Access Trail

N

Amherst Sreet

TO SOUTH HADLEY

0    0.25    0.5

MILES

T

Bachelor Sreet

Riding on a rooted trail. Holyoke Range State Park, Holyoke, Massachusetts.

Hadley, Amherst, South Hadley, and other surrounding towns. Atkins Farms, just 1.1 miles north of the visitor center, has food and drink, including a deli bar, bakery shop, and fresh produce.

**Hazards:** Watch for occasional hikers and announce your presence when approaching them from behind. Expect some bugs, especially in the moister southern part of the forest.

**Rescue index:** You will be around 1.5 miles from a traveled road on secluded trails.

**Land status:** Trails and old roads in a state park and local conservation land.

**Maps:** A map is available from the Department of Environmental Management (see Appendix). Many new trail signs were added to the park in 1998 (with a grant from a regional mountain bike organization). They will help first-time visitors to the park avoid getting lost. Still, a compass is always helpful.

**Finding the trail:** From I-91, take Exit 19, onto MA 9 east (from the south, I-91 is Exit 4 on the Massachusetts Turnpike.) After 0.8 mile on MA 9 east and after crossing the bridge over the Connecticut River, turn right at a sign for MA 47 South/South Hadley. After 1.6 miles, turn left onto Bay Road, and after 2.9 miles, right onto MA 116. After 1.1 miles, you will reach the Notch Visitor Center on the left.

There are two mountain biking trailheads into the park (see map). To reach the southern one, continue southward on MA 116 past the visitor center for 1 mile, and turn left toward MA 202/Granby on Amherst Street. Then turn left after 0.4 mile onto Bachelor Street. After 0.6 mile, watch for a brown gate on the left and small pull-offs on either side of the pavement.

To begin at the northern border of the park, keep going straight on Bay Road, instead of right onto MA 116. After 1.3 miles look for a small turnoff area on the right, with the sign, "Holyoke Range Conservation Area." You can also park at the visitor center on MA 116 and ask about riding from there—but do not take the common, heavily eroded hiking trails leaving from the center.

**Sources of additional information:** Holyoke Range State Park (see Appendix). Drop in the Notch Visitor Center at the park headquarters on MA 116.

**Notes on the trail:** You can begin from either a northern or southern trailhead. From the north (on Bay Road), ride into the woods on a jeep road for 0.2 mile, and turn right onto a double-track trail. All Amherst conservation trails are marked with yellow blazes. Soon, at a T junction, turn left on another double-track trail. After climbing, you will reach a three-way junction with the Northside Trail (blue blazes) and a connecting trail to the Robert Frost Trail (orange) to the left. To do a 2.5-mile loop clockwise on the Robert Frost and Northside trails, keep veering to the right at several junctions and watch for the blazings. (*Note:* From the western end of this loop—the left side on the map—you can reach the Notch Visitor Center using a connecting trail. This is not an "official" mountain-bike trail, and park rangers request cyclists not ride all the way to the visitor center, since the final stretch of trail near the center is eroded and heavily used by hikers.)

From the southern trailhead (on Bachelor Street), ride up the jeep road, and after 0.3 mile, you can fork onto either the Upper Access Trail or Lower Access Trail. The lower access trail is clearer, smoother, and flatter—until it veers left onto the Southside (SS) Trail, which becomes progressively more difficult.

Instead, taking the Upper Access Trail, after 1.2 miles, you can watch for a left turn onto a single-track trail—designed specially for mountain bikers. This is a challenging 0.3-mile trail. You can take it to do a loop onto the Lower Access Trail.

Otherwise, continue on the Upper Access Trail, which soon forks onto one of two trails (Southside and Swamp trails) heading northward and connecting up with the Cliff Side Trail and access to the Robert Frost/Northside loop.

# RIDE 12  ERVING STATE FOREST

This fairly challenging 14-mile ride weaves through light woods for several miles on sometimes steep dirt roads and rugged single-track trails. Then it leaves the forest, first picking up a narrow jeep road, then a two-wheel-drive dirt road through the countryside, an overgrown single-track trail, and finally a short climb on a paved road back to the beach and parking lot. You can create shorter rides out of this one—the forest has many possible loops.

This ride begins by climbing on a double-track trail, which might be overgrown in places. Then you descend to a field full of brilliantly colored wildflowers in summer. You reenter the woods and climb to a high point (where you can find blueberries in July and August).

Laurel Lake at the trailhead has a popular swimming beach, with a bathhouse and a concession stand.

More trails and old roads can be found in three nearby state forests: Warwick, Northfield, and Wendell.

**General location:** Town of Erving, just off Massachusetts Highway 2, about 10 miles east of Interstate 91 and Greenfield.

**Elevation change:** This route includes plenty of climbing and descending, with a couple of flat stretches in the middle. You will begin at 800 feet, climb to 1,050 feet, descend steadily to 600 feet, climb again to 1,100 feet, descend to 700 feet, climb to 900 feet, descend to 700 feet, and climb to 800 feet. Total

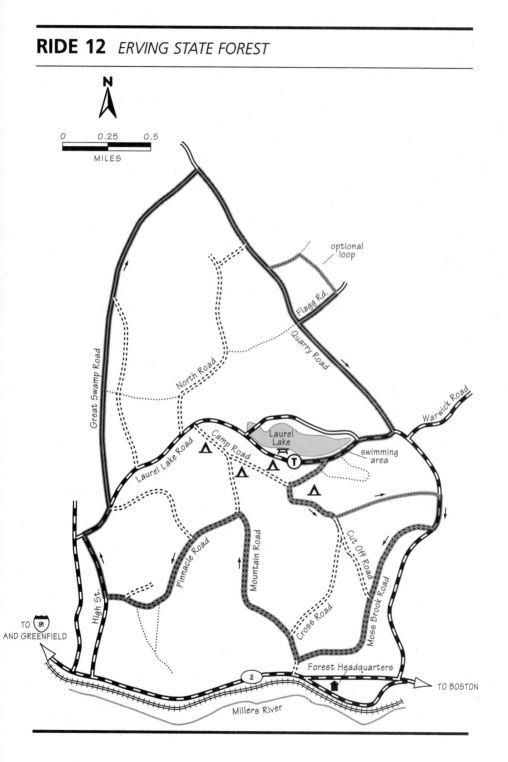

elevation gain is 2,100 feet. There are two flatter sections on Great Swamp and Quarry roads.

**Seasons:** Late spring through late fall.

**Services:** Water and restrooms are available at Laurel Lake near the trailhead. The forest also has many campsites. All other services are found along MA 2 and in Greenfield, 10 miles to the west.

**Hazards:** Watch out for loose terrain on some of the steeper roads, and some hidden obstructions on the grassy, overgrown sections of the trails.

**Rescue index:** At most you will be about 2 miles from assistance.

**Land status:** State forest roads and trails.

**Maps:** Trail maps are available at the main parking lot next to Laurel Lake. Also Erving Variety Store on MA 2, just outside the forest, may carry topographical maps.

**Finding the trail:** Turn north off MA 2 in Erving at brown signs for the state forest. Fork right onto Swamp Road, then Laurel Lake Road, and after about 2.5 miles you will pass Laurel Lake on the left. There are parking areas on the left along the lake at picnic sites—before you reach the parking lot at the beach, which costs a modest fee.

**Sources of additional information:** Erving State Forest (see Appendix).

**Notes on the trail:** This ride weaves in and out of the forest, using a number of secluded trails as well as dirt and paved roads. A map of the area around the forest might also be helpful.

Just before you reach the main parking lot at Laurel Lake, take a sharp right turn up steep Camp Road. After climbing for 0.2 mile, you reach gated Cut Off Road on the left, which heads uphill and south into the woods. Take this jeep road, and fork left at the first junction. (Or to do a somewhat shorter and simpler ride, fork right, staying on Cut Off Road.) Continue downhill and fork right at the next junction onto a single-track trail. You will come out on a paved rural road near another parking area on the border of the state forest.

Turn right on the paved road, and after less than a half mile, just before crossing a large bridge, fork right onto gated, overgrown Moss Brook Road, heading uphill. Then veer right onto a wider, sandy road. Ride past a sand pit, veer right on the road, and you will enter a forest equipment "graveyard." Turn sharply up a steep dirt road on the right, Mountain Road.

When you begin going downhill, turn left onto Pinnacle Road, another dirt woods road. (You can keep going on Mountain Road for a shorter ride.) Descend for a little more than a mile, and turn right at a three-way intersection, coming out on paved High Street. Turn right onto High Street and reach a T junction with Laurel Lake Road. Turn right again, and just before the sign for entering the state forest, fork left uphill onto unsigned Great Swamp Road.

A quiet road through sunlit woods. Erving, Massachusetts.

Follow this flat, narrow road for 2.5 miles, until it comes out on two-wheel-drive dirt Quarry Road. After just over a mile on Quarry Road, you will pass a brown gate at an open field on the left with a trail-use sign at it. You can take the trail behind this gate for an optional loop or else continue on Quarry Road.

To do the optional loop, turn left into the field and follow a grassy road past a logging clearing on the right. You soon reach a fork. Turn right and ride for less than a mile, coming out on dirt Flagg Road. Turn right and ride for a little more than a mile, rejoining Quarry Road.

Then turn left (south) on Quarry Road and descend steadily; you will soon reach an intersection with paved Laurel Lake Road, and a sign for the state forest. Turn right and climb steeply to the east side of Laurel Lake, forking left around the lake to return to the parking lot.

# RIDE 13 BIRCH HILL MANAGEMENT AREA

According to local cyclists, this secluded, yet well-maintained region in northcentral Massachusetts contains more than 100 miles of old dirt roads and trails. This easy-to-moderate 9-mile ride links three loops in it: two grassy single-track trails and a longer loop using double-track trails. All three run along rivers, and they're connected by a mile or so of secluded dirt roads. You can head west and north of this ride for more trails on generally hillier terrain. (For an easier ride in this area, see Ride 14.)

This area is actually known by three different names: Birch Hill Management Area, Lake Denison, and Otter River State Forest. Whichever you prefer, it's a well-kept secret among local mountain bikers. There's also swimming and camping at popular Denison Lake, as well as rentals of mountain bikes, canoes, and kayaks.

**General location:** Just north of the town of Winchendon, off U.S. Highway 202, around 7 miles north of Massachusetts Highway 2.

**Elevation change:** The terrain is quite flat, with occasional short climbs and descents.

**Seasons:** You can ride here in four seasons, with some mud in the spring.

**Services:** All services are available in Gardner and Fitchburg to the south, including O'Neil's Bicycle Shop on Main Street in downtown Gardner.

**Hazards:** Watch out for occasional horseback riders and motorized vehicles on the two-wheel-drive dirt roads. As always, wear some brightly colored clothing in hunting season, from around late October through December.

**Rescue index:** At most you will be about 1 mile from assistance.

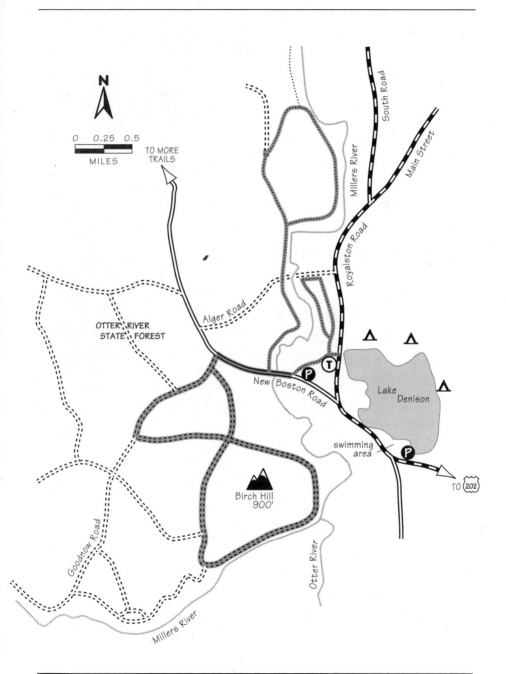

Not all rocks can be hopped. Winchendon, Massachusetts.

**Land status:** Public trails and town roads.

**Maps:** A map is available at the Otter River State Forest headquarters on US 202, just before the turn into the Denison Lake area. John's Sport Shop on Main Street in Gardner stocks maps of this and other riding areas in central Massachusetts.

**Finding the trail:** On MA 2 from the west, take Exit 19 onto US 202 north. On MA 2 from the east, take MA 68 in Gardner toward Baldwinville. After 5 miles, turn right onto US 202 north in Baldwinville. After about 1.5 miles, you will pass a large brown sign for Otter River State Forest, which is another trailhead into this area. Continue on and turn left at the next brown sign, "Lake Denison Recreational Area." Then fork left through an open gate, veer right, and you will reach the parking area at Lake Denison. You can pay and park at the lake or continue along the paved road around the lake and park at turnoffs.

**Sources of additional information:** Otter River State Forest (see Appendix).

**Notes on the trail:** This ride is made up of three loops, linked by a dirt road (New Boston Road). *Loop 1:* Ride clockwise around the lake on the paved road until you reach the Lake Denison boat launching ramp on the right (or you can park across from it). Across from the launching site, turn onto a wide trail. Then bear right and pick up another wide trail paralleling paved Royalston Road on the right. At a junction with a trail on the left, continue straight on a grassier trail to do a counterclockwise loop. You will reach a wide dirt road. Turn left on it, and when you see the river on the right, fork left into the woods. You are now doubling back. When you reach a wider trail, turn right again, and you'll reach unpaved New Boston Road.

*Loop 2:* Turn right on New Boston Road, cross a bridge, and after a few hundred feet, turn right onto a grassy trail at a gate. Ride through a clearing and next to the river (on the right). Stay on the trail next to the river.

Now you have several choices: to do a shorter loop (see map), keep riding farther north along the river on a narrower, more secluded trail, or fork left onto a rugged old road (Wetmore Road) that comes out at New Boston Road after a couple of miles. Or explore both options.

*Loop 3:* Turn right on New Boston Road and left at the junction with unpaved Goodnow Road. Almost immediately, turn left onto a double-track trail and cross a brook on a concrete bridge. At a four-way unpaved intersection, fork left onto narrow Swamp River Road. You will begin riding next to Millers River on the left.

After another half mile or so, fork right. (The left fork will lead to more trails near Birch Hill Dam.) After another half mile or so, turn left at the same four-way intersection you approached from the other direction. You will reach a gate at Goodnow Road. Turn right and rejoin New Boston Road, and right again to return to Lake Denison. You can turn left on Goodnow Road or left on New Boston Road to explore more mapped and unmapped secluded roads and trails.

# RIDE 14 *LAKE DENISON AREA*

This easy 8.5-mile "hybrid" ride explores uninhabited and inhabited country-side, using mainly scenic dirt roads. About 5 miles of the ride use two-wheel-drive and four-wheel-drive dirt roads, with another 3 miles on patchy asphalt. At times, you can feel like you're in Vermont, cruising through a landscape of grassy fields, light woods, and wetlands along a river.

Beginning at popular Lake Denison, you take a secluded, hard-packed dirt road with some more rugged sections. Then you cruise through the inhabited countryside before reentering the Birch Hill Management Area on a shady asphalt road bordered by a stone wall.

According to local cyclists, this area has more than 100 miles of old dirt roads and trails. Several trails and roads turn off New Boston Road. (This ride can be linked with the Ride 13.)

**General location:** Just north of Winchendon, off U.S. Highway 202, about 7 miles north of Massachusetts Highway 2.

**Elevation change:** The terrain is relatively flat, with occasional short climbs and descents.

**Seasons:** This can be a four-season ride.

**Services:** All services are available in Fitchburg and Gardner to the south, including O'Neil's Bicycle Shop on Main Street in Gardner. There is camping and swimming at Denison Lake, as well as mountain bike, canoe, and kayak rentals.

**Hazards:** Watch for traffic on the active town roads.

**Rescue index:** You will be on traveled roads.

**Land status:** Town roads.

**Maps:** A good road map will show this route. Also, a map of the area is available at the Otter River State Forest headquarters on US 202, just before the turn into the Lake Denison area. John's Sport Shop on Main Street in Gardner stocks maps of this and other riding sites in central Massachusetts.

**Finding the trail:** On MA 2 from the west, take Exit 19 onto US 202 north. On MA 2 from the east, take MA 68 in Gardner toward Baldwinville. After 5 miles, turn right on US 202 north in Baldwinville. After another 1.5 miles, you will pass a large brown sign for Otter River State Forest. Go past the sign, and turn left at a second sign: "Lake Denison Recreational Area." Fork left through an open gate. Then veer right and you will reach the parking area at Lake Denison. You can either pay and park, or continue along the paved road and park at turnoffs along the lake.

# RIDE 14 *LAKE DENISON AREA*

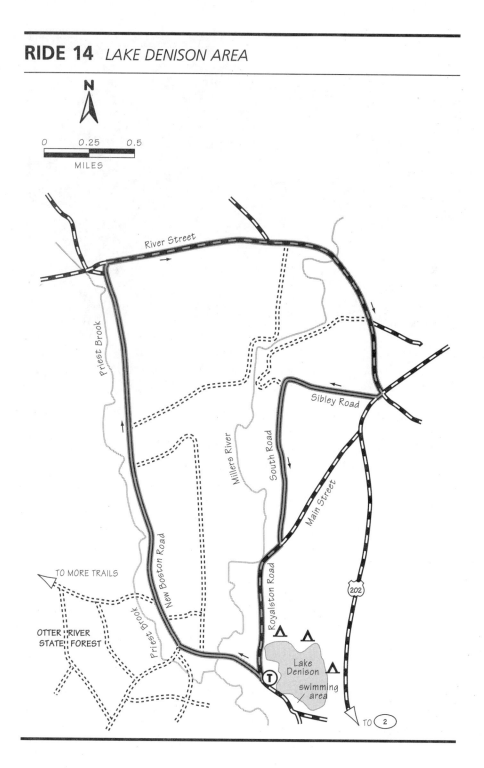

N

0        0.25        0.5

MILES

River Street

Priest Brook

Sibley Road

Millers River

South Road

Main Street

New Boston Road

TO MORE TRAILS

Priest Brook

OTTER RIVER
STATE FOREST

Royalston Road

202

Lake
Denison

swimming
area

T

TO 2

Cruising through a pastoral landscape. Winchendon, Massachusetts.

**Sources of additional information:** Otter River State Forest (see Appendix).

**Notes on the trail:** Head north from Lake Denison on unpaved New Boston Road. (You will pass dirt roads heading off into the woods—more riding possibilities.) After 3 miles, you reach a T junction on a paved road at the Winchendon and Royalston town border. Turn right, and after about 2 miles, fork right at the next major intersection. You will reach a stop sign on paved US 202. Turn right, and immediately right again onto Sibley Road. At the next fork, turn left (heading south). You will pass a sign announcing the Birch Hill Management Area. When you reach an intersection, turn right onto paved Royalston Road and return to Lake Denison. (Again, you can explore the dirt roads on the right.)

# RIDE 15  *BRIMFIELD STATE FOREST*

This moderate 6.5-mile ride explores a half-dozen secluded woods roads in a quiet, pleasant forest. About half of the roads are wide, flat, and hard-packed, while the other half are steeper double-track trails, with some loose rock. (One can do easier loops by using the flatter, smoother roads.)

Maples, ashes, and oaks share the woodscape here with stands of tall pine trees. At the junction of three roads, there is also a large pond with an old campsite at it.

The forest has a large adjoining picnic and swimming area, Dean Pond, on Sutcliffe Mill Road, farther along Massachusetts Highway 20. Although the official trail map does not show trails linking the forest to the pond, several trailheads head west toward Sutcliffe Mill Road. There's also an ice-cream stand at a scenic dairy farm farther along MA 20; follow the signs.

You also might want to visit one of the most famous reconstructed Colonial-era villages in New England, Sturbridge Village, which holds special public events, particularly in the fall. It's located 10 miles west of the forest.

**General location:** The town of Brimfield, between Worcester and Springfield, about 60 miles west of Boston.

**Elevation change:** Most of the ride is flat, but there are several short climbs on loose terrain.

**Seasons:** This can be a four-season ride. The roads are well-drained, which makes them less muddy in the spring.

**Services:** There are restrooms, water, picnicking, and swimming at the Dean Pond area from Memorial Day to Labor Day. There's a modest fee to park and swim at the pond. All other services are available along MA 20.

**Hazards:** Be prepared for some downhill stretches of loose rock and minor obstructions.

**Rescue index:** You will be about 1 mile from assistance on secluded roads.

**Land status:** State forest and town roads.

**Maps:** Trail maps are available at the Dean Pond area.

**Finding the trail:** From Interstate 84, just a half mile south of I-90 (the Massachusetts Turnpike), take Exit 8 onto MA 20 west. A couple of miles west of Brimfield and a half mile after MA 20 becomes four-lane, turn left onto Dearth Hill Road. (If you reach a sign for the state forest, you just passed this access road.) After a half mile or so, just before a pond on the left, turn left into an unpaved parking area.

**Sources of additional information:** Brimfield State Forest (see Appendix).

# RIDE 15 *BRIMFIELD STATE FOREST*

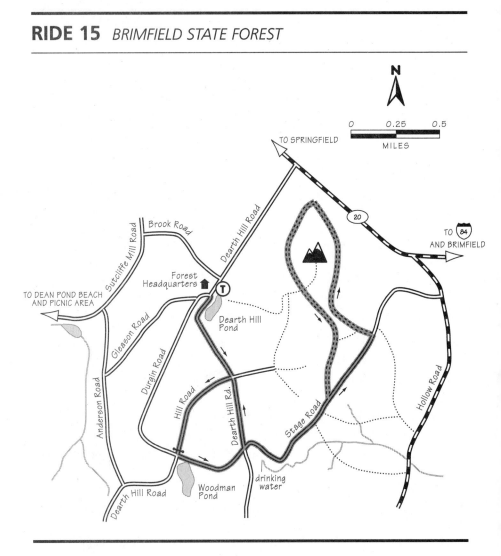

**Notes on the trail:** From the parking lot, ride up Dearth Hill Road for a short distance, past the forest headquarters gate and building complex on the right. Continue on the road for about 0.5 mile, and turn right onto Hill Road. (This road is narrower and not quite as hard-packed.) Follow it for just over 0.5 mile to an intersection with a forest gate. Turn left onto Woodman Road and you will pass the pond on your right. (There is a trail around the pond, which becomes overgrown after about a half mile.)

Then you intersect another dirt road; make a dogleg turn to the left and right across it, onto Stage Road. When you reach a small fork in the trail, stay to the right. (The steep road on the left is where the ride will come out.) At the next junction, after about a half mile, turn left onto another woods road, and almost immediately turn right at the next fork.

You will descend until you almost reach a private yard (on MA 20). Veer left on the trail, staying in the woods, as it reverses direction and climbs. Then veer right at the next fork, and arrive back at Stage Road. Turn right and ride back to the intersection with Dearth Hill Road. Turn right again and ride to the parking area.

# RIDE 16 *LEOMINSTER STATE FOREST*

This 7-mile ride connects four rugged woods roads through a quiet, scenic woodland. These abandoned dirt roads are often no wider than a double-track trail, with plenty of exposed bedrock, eroded stretches, loose terrain, and an occasional shallow water hole.

This 4,000-acre forest is a varied and handsome habitat—a mix of hardwoods and softwoods, mountain laurel bushes, low-level ferns and mosses, and boulders strewn around. In places it looks like a New England version of a Japanese garden. The forest also has a swimming beach and large picnic areas near the trailhead.

**General location:** On Massachusetts Highway 31, a few miles south of Fitchburg and 40 miles west of Boston.

**Elevation change:** The ride climbs gently from 750 feet to 950 feet, then descends to about 700 feet and climbs back.

**Seasons:** This can be a four-season ride if there is little snow and not too much wetness in the spring.

**Services:** All services are available in Fitchburg, including Gamache's Cyclery.

**Hazards:** None.

**Rescue index:** At most you will be about 1 mile from a traveled road.

**Land status:** Roads and trails in a state forest.

**Maps:** You can pick up a map at the forest headquarters on MA 31, about 1.5 miles north of the trailhead.

**Finding the trail:** From the north, on MA 2 take Exit 28 (MA 31), turning onto MA 31 south. After a mile, you will pass the forest headquarters on the right. After another 1.2 miles, you pass the main parking lot at a large pond on the

## RIDE 16 *LEOMINSTER STATE FOREST*

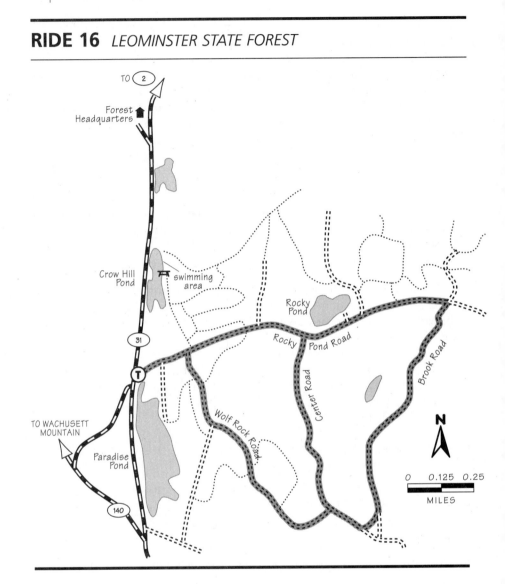

left. Continue for another half mile to the mountain biking trailhead at Rocky Pond Road on the left. From the south, take Interstate 190 to MA 140, to MA 31 north.

**Sources of additional information:** Leominster State Forest (see Appendix).

**Notes on the trail:** These roads are easy to follow in any direction you want. This forest also has miles of winding single-track trails (created by off-road motorcyclists), many of them located north of Rocky Pond Road.

Heading into a forest. Leominster State Forest, Leominster, Massachusetts.

Biking is not allowed on the hiking trails on the west side of MA 31. (Riders should be courteous and slow down around hikers on all the trails.)

For a nearby climb to a scenic overlook on dirt and asphalt roads, check out Mt. Wachusett (2,006 feet) at Wachusett Mountain State Reservation in Princeton.

# RIDE 17  *DOUGLAS STATE FOREST*

This woodland is a favorite mountain biking destination—it's conveniently located in the corner of all three states in southern New England. The moderate 12-mile ride in this book combines both loops and out-and-back sections in this 4,500-acre forest.

About half of the 30-plus miles of trails here are loose-gravel and dirt roads built during the 1930s by the Civilian Conservation Corps. This massive public works project employed 95,000 men and boys during the Depression to build hundreds of miles of roads and trails in parks and forests throughout

Massachusetts. Mountain bikers are now benefiting from these innovative federal projects.

The rest of the trails in this forest are double- and singletrack—some grassy, others covered with plenty of rocks. And a rail-trail—a flat, wide cinder path—intersects the forest, extending in either direction.

In the woods, you'll find oak, ash, and pine trees alternating with wetlands and grassy clearings. In many places, the ground is also strewn with granite boulders and supports the occasional rare wild orchid. As you ride, look for blueberry bushes, which ripen in August; tiny, waxy wintergreen plants, so named because they stay green all winter and smell like wintergreen gum when crushed; and tall flowering rhododendron bushes.

At the southern end of the forest, there's popular Wallum Lake, with a swimming beach, boating, lawns, and shaded picnic areas. At the northern end of the forest, at a former mill site near Wallis Pond, a stream still tumbles over a dam.

**General location:** The town of Douglas, in the corner of Massachusetts, Connecticut, and Rhode Island.

**Elevation change:** The terrain is relatively flat, with a few climbs and descents on loose gravel.

**Seasons:** Any time between mid-May and late fall is good. Autumn offers colorful foliage.

**Services:** There are water fountains, spigots, and restrooms at Wallum Lake. All other services are available in Douglas.

**Hazards:** Be ready to switch riding conditions from hard-packed dirt to loose gravel and steep tricky sections on narrower trails. Watch out for horseback riders and hikers, especially near Wallum Lake. Expect some mosquitoes in the spring.

**Rescue index:** At most you will be about 1 mile from a traveled road.

**Land status:** State forest roads and trails.

**Maps:** There is a trail map on a board at Wallum Lake. For a copy, contact the Department of Environmental Management (see Appendix).

**Finding the trail:** Depending on where you want to begin riding, you can park at one of three areas. To reach a mountain-bike parking area on Massachusetts Highway 16, from either Douglas (to the east) or Interstate 395 (Exit 2) and Webster (to the west), look for a kiosk and gated trailhead on the southern side of the road after about 4 miles. A parking area for the northern half of the forest is off Wallis Street north of MA 16. The main forest parking lot is at Wallum Lake. On busy weekends, rangers ask that mountain bikers use the parking area on MA 16.

**Sources of additional information:** Douglas State Forest (see Appendix).

# RIDE 17 *DOUGLAS STATE FOREST*

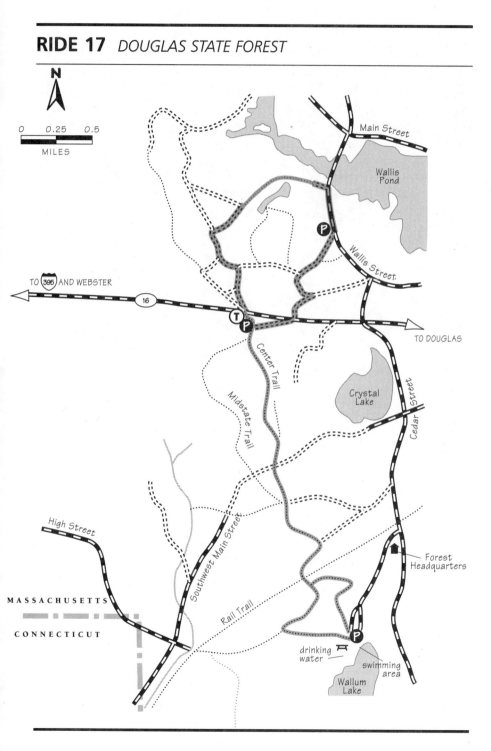

N

0    0.25    0.5
MILES

Main Street

Wallis Pond

Wallis Street

TO 395 AND WEBSTER

16

TO DOUGLAS

Center Trail

Midstate Trail

Crystal Lake

Cedar Street

High Street

Southwest Main Street

MASSACHUSETTS

CONNECTICUT

Rail Trail

Forest Headquarters

drinking water

swimming area

Wallum Lake

Laying a new water bar across a trail. KRISTINA HOLLY PHOTO

**Notes on the trail:** You can explore trails heading either north or south in this elongated forest. The first half of the ride here begins at Wallum Lake and heads north to MA 16.

*From Wallum Lake to MA 16:* From the picnic area at Wallum Lake, ride away from the lake on a smooth, sandy road behind the bathhouse, passing a cabin on the right. Soon you will pass a sign for the Cedar Swamp Trail, a popular hiking loop. At the next junction, fork left onto a narrower double-track trail. Then turn right onto a trail marked "Coffee House Loop" (another popular hiking trail). Cross a wooden bridge and go straight on the wider trail at a fork, where the Coffee House Loop turns right. Almost immediately, you will intersect the rail-trail, which is a sunny, flat, wide, loose-gravel path that you can also take in either direction.

Ride across the rail-trail and begin following the yellow blazes marking the Midstate Trail, an 85-mile-long hiking trail running north-south through Massachusetts. (In about a half mile, you will get off the Midstate Trail, which becomes almost impassable.) After the rail-trail, fork right, then left at an intersection of four gravel roads, and left again at a fork with another gravel road. Then go straight across a four-way intersection of gravel roads (the Midstate Trail heads left).

You reach gravel Southwest Main Street at a gate. Pick up a single-track trail on the other side of the road, and soon veer left on a wider trail, still heading north. This is the Center Trail, which is dotted with rocks. You will come out at a T junction. Turn left and reach paved MA 16.

*From MA 16 to Wallis Pond:* On the other side of MA 16 pick up another woods road, and soon turn left on a dirt and gravel road. At the next fork, you can go straight for a longer ride, or turn right to reach the mill site near Wallis Pond. Turn right and, after cruising on a grassy trail, cross the bridge at the mill site and pick up a dirt road on the left that meets paved Wallis Street. (You can also keep going straight just before the mill site for a scenic ride along Wallis Pond and up a hill.)

Turn right onto paved Wallis Street, and you'll soon reach a parking area and a large brown gate. Turn right onto a gravel road heading into the forest. Take the second left fork onto a narrower double-track trail and then turn right at a T junction with three red blazes on a tree. You will come out at MA 16, near the trailhead.

# RIDE 18 *UPTON STATE FOREST*

Mountain biking has become better and better in this convenient state forest—it's near both Interstates 90 (the Massachusetts Turnpike) and 495, just 30 miles from both Boston, Massachusetts, and Providence, Rhode Island. The rangers here have cut a brand-new single-track trail, which loops for about 3 miles through the northern part of this 2,600-acre forest. Despite its newness, this well-marked trail is relatively free of stumps and other obstructions. Also, many of the major intersections in the forest are marked with helpful brown-and-white wooden signs. The forest welcomes cyclists and remains largely undeveloped.

One can do moderate loops here using the wider, loose-gravel jeep roads, or tackle some of the more rugged double-track trails. Be sure to make a rest stop at tranquil Dean Pond, deep in the forest, and take in the pleasant, light woodscape everywhere: mixed hardwoods, low bushes, and delicate groundcover. Also, at the summit off Park Road, a trail forks to a scenic overlook.

**General location:** Towns of Upton and Hopkinton, 5 miles west of I-495, 8 miles south of I-90 (the Massachusetts Turnpike), 30 miles west of Boston, Massachusetts, and 30 miles north of Providence, Rhode Island.

**Elevation change:** There's a moderate amount of climbing, especially up and down Park Road, which rises steadily from the parking area, then descends toward Hopkinton Road. Loop Road is flatter. The single-track trail loop described in Notes on the trail has several steep but short climbs on it.

**Seasons:** This can be a four-season ride, with some muddy stretches, especially on the trails, in the spring. There's plenty of colorful foliage in the fall and snowmobile-packed trails in the winter.

**Services:** All services are available in Milford to the south, including Milford Bicycle on Main Street, a full-service bike shop with information about mountain biking in the area. There is no drinking water in the forest.

**Hazards:** Be prepared to change riding techniques when switching from the wider jeep roads to the more difficult single-track trails. Also, the forest is patrolled by rangers on horseback, so be prepared to meet and greet them.

**Rescue index:** At most you will be about 1 mile from a traveled road.

**Land status:** Public roads and trails in a state forest.

**Maps:** Maps are stocked in a box at the trailhead. Otherwise, ask at the headquarters near the forest entrance.

**Finding the trail:** Take Exit 21B (West Main Street/Upton) on I-495 (the first exit south of I-90) and head west toward Upton. After 3.5 miles, turn sharply right across from a large pond on the left (Pratt Pond) onto Westboro Road. After another 2 miles, turn right onto Southboro Road, and immediately take the dirt road straight ahead to a forest parking area; the paved road on the right goes to the forest headquarters.

**Sources of additional information:** Upton State Forest (see Appendix).

**Notes on the trail:** There are several options for beginning a ride here. For a mellower loop using the dirt roads, head up Park Road and continue on it, climbing and then descending on loose gravel, or else fork left onto Loop Road, then back on Middle Road or Dean Pond Road.

Single-track enthusiasts should be sure to do the excellent new trails in the northern part of the forest. They're easy to follow. First, head back out the access road, and turn sharply right onto paved Spring Street. Within a hundred feet or so, look for a trailhead into the woods on the left, marked with a blue arrow. This is the beginning of the Rabbit Run Trail. Then just follow the blue arrows, as the trail soon crosses paved Westboro Road and winds through the forest. This trail connects with the Old Hopkinton Spring Trail and the Mammoth Rock Trail; after a short stretch on the Grouse Trail, you come out on Loop Road. From there, you can either return to the trailhead or turn left and explore other areas of the forest.

The Whistling Cave Trail is fairly difficult, as are trails off Park Road to the west.

# RIDE 18 *UPTON STATE FOREST*

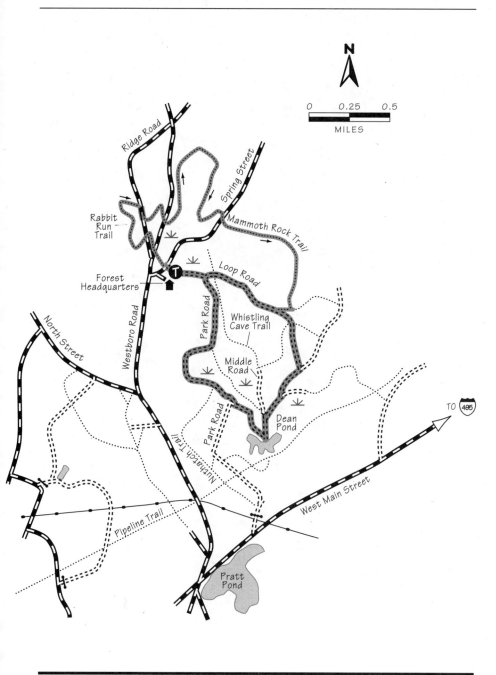

A new single-track trail. Upton State Forest, Upton, Massachusetts.

# RIDE 19 *AYER-PEPPERELL LINE*

This former railroad bed is now an 8.5-mile multi-use path running through three handsome small towns. By spring 1999, this rail-trail is supposed to be extended another 1.5 miles, to the New Hampshire border, and it will also be redesigned. The new trail will be expanded into a 17-foot-wide corridor, with a 10-foot-wide paved section and a 7-foot-wide unpaved section.

From either end, this ultra-flat trail quickly leaves civilization, entering an uninhabited landscape of light woods and fields. On the southern half, between Ayer and Groton, it runs for a short distance along a secluded body of water, where you might see geese. Near its northern end, in Pepperell, it borders a modest 500-acre state forest with a large pond and tall pine trees lining the path. (The state forest offers some dirt roads and trails that intersect the rail-trail.) The trail also has two short tunnels on it.

You can do a 17-mile out-and-back ride on the trail, or else loop around through the scenic countryside on paved Massachusetts Highway 111.

**General location:** Towns of Ayer, Groton, and Pepperell, to the New Hampshire border.

**Elevation change:** Flat. (Railroad beds were never inclined more than two degrees.)

**Seasons:** Year-round, with coolness and color in the fall.

**Services:** All services are available just off the trail in Ayer, Groton, and Pepperell. A block from the trail in Groton are a bakery, pharmacy, and other stores—as well as some grand houses for sightseeing.

**Hazards:** Be sure to scan for traffic at the cross streets; motorists do not always expect cyclists to come out of the woods.

**Rescue index:** At most you will be about 0.25 mile from a traveled road.

**Land status:** A former railroad bed now a public right-of-way.

**Maps:** A detailed road map will show the surrounding roads.

**Finding the trail:** You can begin in Ayer, Pepperell, or at the midpoint in Groton. From the south, on MA 2, take the exit for both MA 110 and MA 111/Ayer/Groton. After 1.8 miles, follow the signs around the rotary for Ayer. After another 2.5 miles, you will reach downtown Ayer. At the junction of Main and Park streets, pick up the trail just behind a parking lot on the north side of the street. Coming from the east, take Interstate 495 to Exit 30 (Littleton/Ayer).

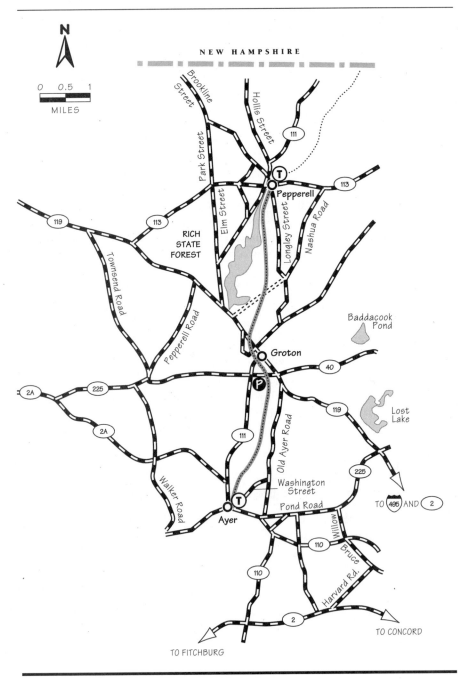

A tunnel on a rail-trail. Ayer, Massachusetts.

In Groton, the trail is just one block off MA 119, just south of the junction of MA 111 and MA 119.

In Pepperell, the trail crosses at the junction of MA 113 and Longley Street in East Pepperell, opposite a row of stores and a gas station (with an air hose).

**Sources of additional information:** Pepperell Selectman's Office or the Department of Environmental Management (see Appendix).

**Notes on the trail:** At the trail's halfway point is the handsome town of Groton. If you prefer doing a loop instead of an out-and-back ride, you can take MA 111 from Groton to Ayer, a scenic rural highway that's almost entirely downhill heading southward. You pick it up just off Main Street in Groton.

# Eastern Massachusetts

## RIDE 20  *LOWELL-DRACUT-TYNGSBORO STATE PARK*

This under-used 1,150-acre forest has 15 miles or so of trails and roads just made for mountain biking. Its southern section is laced with a network of trails that climb over rocks and roots through a pleasant woodscape. By using several dirt roads (and one paved stretch), you can also circumvent the large marsh at the center of the park.

In the northwest section of the forest, there's a piney woods that is used by local Native American tribes for powwow ceremonies. These gatherings include music, singing, dancing, crafts, and foods. Held at various times and places throughout New England in the summer and fall, powwows are often open to the public.

**General location:** Just north of Lowell, off Massachusetts Highway 113, and 30 miles north of Boston.

**Elevation change:** The terrain is relatively flat, with a few short climbs.

**Seasons:** Any time between late spring and late fall is good. Expect some mud in the spring.

**Services:** All services are available in Lowell, Dracut, and Tyngsboro, and along MA 113.

**Hazards:** Yield to the occasional horseback rider.

**Rescue index:** At most you will be about a half mile from a well-traveled road.

**Land status:** State park roads and trails.

**Maps:** Call or write the Department of Environmental Management for a map (see Appendix).

**Finding the trail:** From MA 3 (about 10 miles north of Interstate 495), take Exit 34, and turn right toward Tyngsboro. After 1 mile, fork left at the light, and immediately right across a large bridge. Almost immediately, fork right onto Sherburne Avenue (*not* the sharp right turn onto MA 113 east). After 3.3 miles, just past a modern-looking church building, turn left onto Trotting Park Road. You will soon see gated trailheads on the right side of the road. Park at a trailhead, or go about 1 mile to a parking area.

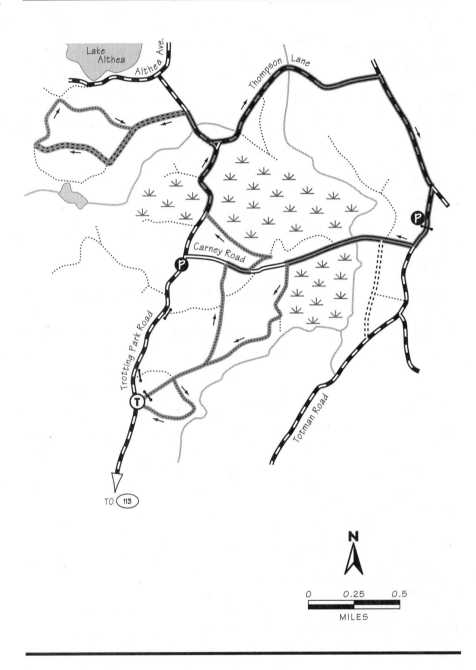

Lake Althea

Althea Ave.

Thompson Lane

Carney Road

Trotting Park Road

Totman Road

TO 113

N

0    0.25    0.5

MILES

An active Native American powwow site. Lowell-Dracut-Tyngsboro State Park, Lowell, Massachusetts.

**Sources of additional information:** Lowell-Dracut-Tyngsboro State Park (see Appendix).

**Notes on the trail:** The 8-mile loop on the map shows one possible ride through the forest, beginning at a gated trailhead on Trotting Park Road. The forest is divided roughly in half by unpaved Carney Road. South of it, there is a network of single-track trails.

On the north side of Carney Road, you can pick up a trail that runs along the southwest edge of the marsh, coming out on asphalt Trotting Park Road, which is another orienting road in the forest. At a three-way intersection on this road, you can fork left, cross a small stream, and almost immediately turn left into another section of the forest, which has a narrow road through it, several trails, and well-maintained campsites (used by Native Americans).

If you turn right at the three-way fork on Trotting Park Road, you can take Thompson Lane, until it leaves the forest and becomes a trail through an inhabited landscape, coming out on a paved road. Turn right, then soon fork right onto paved Totman Road, which becomes unpaved at a gate. Turn right onto unpaved Carney Road. After passing a large marsh on the right, watch for trails on the left that will take you back to Trotting Park Road.

# RIDE 21 *GREAT BROOK FARM STATE PARK*

This is the kind of place to bring someone you want to introduce to the sport of mountain biking. The 935-acre park has 20 miles or so of scenic trails rolling through open fields, woods, and wetlands. You're never far from a trailhead either—and there's a homemade ice-cream stand with picnic tables at a small pond for post-ride treats. The countryside here looks like southern Vermont, with well-maintained farms and an occasional pond harboring geese.

The moderate 8-mile ride in this book will first take you past wetlands, where peeper frogs call insistently in the spring. Along the Woodchuck Trail (to the east), you can then cruise past hundreds of bright-green pine saplings growing under their cathedral-like progenitors. White pines, the region's tallest indigenous tree, once dominated the New England landscape. Then the British discovered that they made world-class ship masts. It was the first exploitation of the natural North American landscape.

The main trails at Great Brook are pine-covered and grassy double-track. More challenging single-track trails branch off them, and a wide, rugged gas pipeline trail runs along the northern border.

A short ride across paved Lowell Road and onto Curve Street to the west leads you to a colorful cranberry bog—the northernmost one in Massachusetts—with a trail around it.

**General location:** Town of Carlisle, about 12 miles north of Concord, 25 miles northwest of Boston.

**Elevation change:** This terrain is relatively flat, with small hills. Some of the single-track trails have short, steep ascents, and the pipeline to the north has longer climbs and descents on it.

**Seasons:** Summer and fall are best. Winter is usually reserved for cross-country skiers.

**Services:** There are restrooms, water, and ice cream at the trailhead. All other services are available in nearby towns like Carlisle, Lincoln, Bedford, and Concord. The Lincoln Guide Service, a full-service bike shop in Lincoln, about 10 miles south of the ride, has a lot of maps and information on mountain biking in this area. It also rents bikes.

**Hazards:** This park is popular among hikers and horseback riders, as well as cross-country skiers. Be prepared to slow down.

**Rescue index:** You will be no more than a half mile from a paved road.

**Land status:** Trails in a state park.

**Maps:** Maps are stocked in a box at the main parking lot.

Riding beside a cornfield. Great Brook Farm State Park, Carlisle, Massachusetts.

**Finding the trail:** From the south, take Lowell Road out of Concord heading north toward Carlisle. In the center of Carlisle, veer left toward Chelmsford. After about 1.5 miles, you pass the regional headquarters for the Department of Environmental Management, then the park headquarters on the left. Turn right soon after the headquarters at a sign for the park. After a third of a mile, you will reach the large gravel parking lot on the left at the farm pond.

**Sources of additional information:** Great Brook Farm State Park (see Appendix).

**Notes on the trail:** Fanning out from the main parking area at the pond and farm, trails lead in several directions. The ride on this map links up several of these areas. To explore the woods south of North Road, just pick up a double-track trail across the road from the parking lot. At a T junction, turn left and reach the Pine Point Loop. Or turn right, cross a small bridge, pass a field on the right, and after going downhill, turn up a single-track trail on the right. This is Heart Break Ridge Trail, which becomes a pine needle-covered single-track that loops back on a more technical trail.

On the other side of North Road you can pick up a wide double-track trail, Woodchuck Trail. There you will pass an old mill site, cabin, stone bridge,

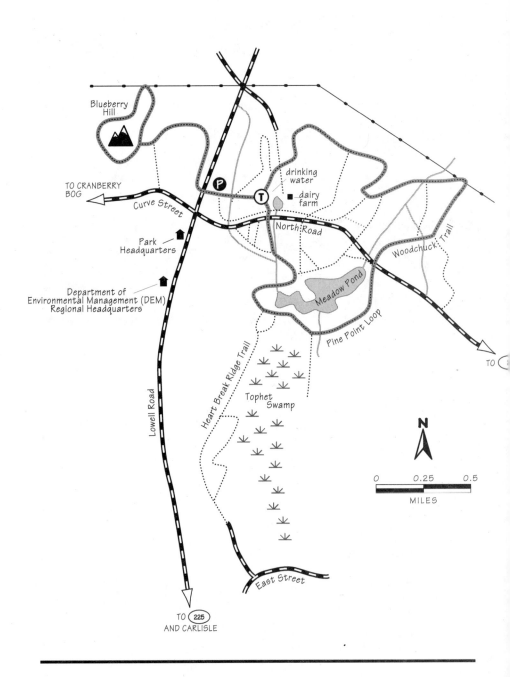

stone walls, and giant pine trees. You can try short loops off the trail, continue north to link up with the pipeline trail, or veer left and reach trails heading back toward the farm through fields.

Finally, there's good riding west of Lowell Road, toward Blueberry Hill. From the hill, you can also pick up the pipeline (to the north), and head west on it, reach Martin Street, turn left on it, and pick up trails on the right toward the cranberry bog.

# RIDE 22 *STOW TOWN FOREST*

This compact forest is a convenient riding site in the suburbs west of Boston. It's ideal for either a day-trip or an evening excursion. Within its 325 acres, you can explore 10 or so miles of old dirt lanes, double-track trails, and several miles of single-track trails, rolling along the quiet Assabet River and ascending and descending Gardner Hill. You can do both easy and moderate loops. Although many of the colored tree blazings have faded along the trails, the trails themselves remain clear and inviting.

Don't miss the forest for the trails either—this is a classic New England woodscape, with 100-foot-tall pine trees forming an upper canopy, a midlevel of bushes and shrubs, and an understory of new growth and wintergreen plants. The 300-foot Gardner Hill, with its wooded summit of oaks and other hardwood trees, rises in the middle of the forest, which is bordered by the wide Assabet River on one side and a brook and wetland on the other.

Near the river, along a single-track trail, you'll pass some well-kept campfire sites, where local Boy Scouts hold outdoor meetings.

**General location:** The town of Stow, about 20 miles west of Boston.

**Elevation change:** Gently rolling terrain, with one short, steep climb to and descent from a hill.

**Seasons:** Summer and fall are best.

**Services:** All services are available in Stow, along Massachusetts Highway 117 and in nearby towns. Erickson's Ice Cream stand is located 1 mile south on MA 117/62.

**Hazards:** Bring an insect repellent in wetter and hotter conditions. Also, watch for some loose sand at low-lying trail intersections, and a steep downhill stretch on the west side of Gardner Hill—don't hesitate to dismount.

**Rescue index:** You will be about a half mile from a traveled road.

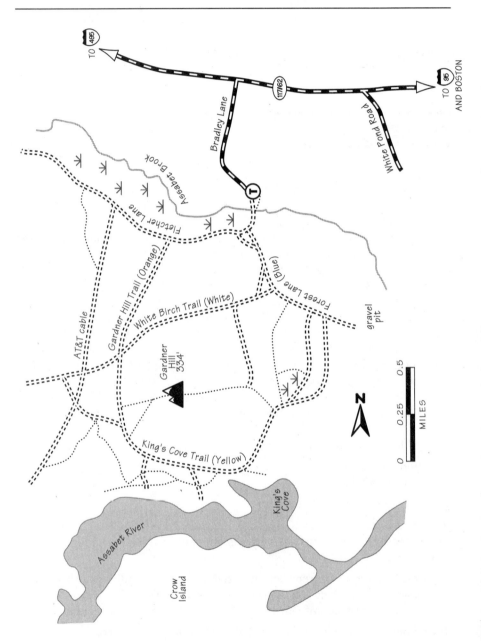

Fork at a tall pine. Stow Town Forest, Stow, Massachusetts.

**Land status:** Roads and trails in a public town forest. (The forest is bordered by private land.)

**Maps:** The map in this book is the best available. You can pick up an "official" map from the Conservation Commission in the Town Building; as of this writing, though, it shows only the major roads.

**Finding the trail:** From the east, take either MA 117 west or MA 62 west (for around three miles in Stow, the two routes merge). Bradley Lane, which heads into the forest, comes up 1.3 miles after MA 62 joins MA 117. Watch for the Stow Shopping Center on the right; 0.2 mile further, turn left onto Bradley Lane (the street sign may be partly obscured by tree branches). From the west, Bradley Lane comes up on the right, 0.7 mile after MA 117 and MA 62 merge. Follow Bradley Lane to a gravel parking area at the trailhead. *Note:* Drive slowly on this narrow road, which has a blind curve and several rural homes on it.

**Sources of additional information:** Stow Conservation Commission (see Appendix).

**Notes on the trail:** One can mix-and-match the jeep roads and wider trails with the single-track trails to create mellower or more challenging loops. Since most of the color-coded blazings on the five main trails are faded (at the time of this writing), you might feel lost at times, but there are distinct junctions and landmarks to orient yourself. For instance, one clearly recognizable feature is the AT&T cable line, with its orange posts and flat, straight path.

Even less-advanced riders should try some of the single-track trails since they offer a close view of the river (south of King's Cove Trail), like Gardner Hill (via the White Birch Trail), and intimate woods. If you climb Gardner Hill, do so from the more gradual eastern side.

# RIDE 23 *HAROLD PARKER STATE FOREST*

This second-oldest state park in Massachusetts has plenty of riding possibilities on about 25 miles of jeep roads and trails. The roads through this 3,000-acre wooded site wind around a half-dozen ponds, while double- and single-track trails cut through deep woods and grassy wetlands, and pass granite outcroppings. Depending on whether you stay on the woods roads or tackle the more challenging trails, a ride can be anywhere from easy to difficult. This moderate 10-mile loop alternates between trails and roads.

The forest is convenient to many cities and towns in northeastern Massachusetts, such as Lowell, Lawrence, Haverhill, Reading, Burlington, and Lynn. It also has almost 100 campsites and a swimming beach on Stearns Pond.

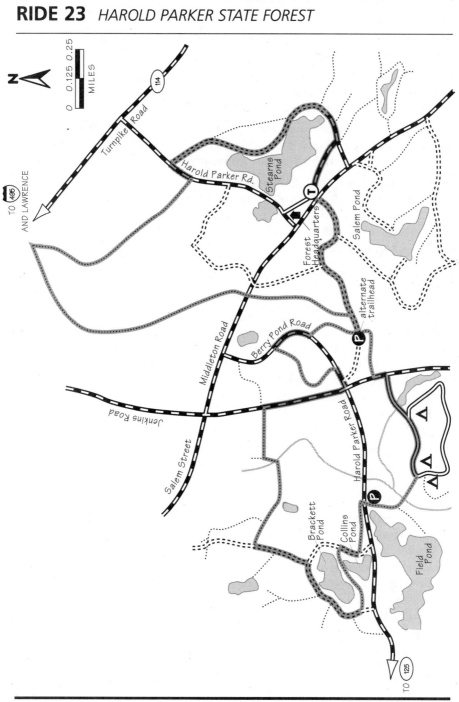

**General location:** Towns of Andover and North Andover, about 25 miles north of Boston.

**Elevation change:** The terrain is relatively flat, with some rolling sections and short climbs.

**Seasons:** Plenty of shade and ponds make this a good summer ride. There is some mud in the spring and, if there's snow in the winter, some trails are used by cross-country skiers. Autumn brings colorful foliage.

**Services:** All services are available in Andover and North Reading, including The Cycle Shop on Massachusetts Highway 62 in North Reading. The state forest also has 92 campsites (mid-April through October, with showers).

**Hazards:** Watch out for hikers and horseback riders, especially around the ponds and trailheads. Also, the terrain sometimes changes abruptly, from wide, flat woods roads to narrow, winding trails, which sometimes cross paved roads.

**Rescue index:** You will always be close to well-traveled roads.

**Land status:** State park roads and trails.

**Maps:** Maps are usually stocked in a box outside park headquarters.

**Finding the trail:** Take Exit 41 on Interstate 93 and turn right onto MA 125 north toward Andover. After 2.5 miles, just past the state police barracks, turn right toward a sign for the state forest. You will pass between two large stone pillars onto Harold Parker Road. Follow the signs for forest headquarters (where trail maps are stocked).

Along the way, you can park at turnoffs at several trailheads along Harold Parker Road, near ponds. There's another parking area just beyond the intersection of Harold Parker and Jenkins roads.

**Sources of additional information:** Harold Parker State Forest (see Appendix).

**Notes on the trail:** Each of the four sections in this spread-out forest contain loops and networks of trails and woods roads that can be connected across paved roads. (Some of the woods roads have short trails branching off them that deadend at private property. If you take one, just double back and pick up the main trail.)

*Shorter loops:* The flat double-back trails around Brackett and Collins ponds in the western part of the forest are easy and scenic. A longer, more challenging trail runs for 3 miles into the northern part of the forest between Middleton and Turnpike roads. The shorter woods road loop inside it is another possibility. A compact network of single-track trails laces the hills just north of Berry Pond Road.

*A long loop:* Begin riding on a jeep road heading southwest just across from the forest headquarters. Turn right at a fork, then left at the next one. You will reach a large gravel parking area (another trailhead). Take a sharp left turn out of the gravel lot onto a single-track trail and you will reach paved Jenkins

Road. Turn left for a few hundred feet on the road and then right onto a paved access road into the forest camping area.

Stay to the right on the access road, watching out for other forest users. At the bottom of the camping area, turn right, ride along Field Pond, and come out on Harold Parker Road. Turn left on the pavement and pick up a double-track trail on the other side of the road. This trail will merge with a wider old road.

You can now circumvent Brackett and Collins ponds, or head north and pick up a trail on the right toward Jenkins Road. Then take single-track trails heading east, a long loop trail northward to Turnpike Road, and finally pick up a woods road around Stearns Pond that leads back to the headquarters.

# RIDE 24 *MAUDSLAY STATE PARK*

This easy 5-mile loop ride weaves along the same paths once trodden by famous New England artists and intellectuals. Maudslay Estate, with its 43 rooms and formal gardens, was a popular meeting place for New England luminaries in the late nineteenth and early twentieth centuries. Poets like John Greenleaf Whittier and mystics like Katherine Tingley, founder of the Theosophical Society, gathered here to commune with nature and put on theatrical events.

Today, you can see the remains of the formal gardens, as well as hundreds of flowering trees and shrubs—mountain laurel, rhododendron, azalea, dogwood, crab apple, roses, and dozens of different wildflowers. A 2-mile trail runs along the grand Merrimack River while other trails weave through pine stands and manicured meadows and across stone bridges.

Although these well-maintained trails (called "carriage roads" because they were first built for horse-drawn carriages) are easy riding, they're varied, with rolling stretches, sharp turns, and occasional rooted terrain. Needless to say, though, this is not a place to "hammer" through. Some animals live in the park, too. Cyclists must stay on the carriage roads.

A few miles east of Maudslay (named after the family's ancestral home in England) is Newburyport, a lively coastal town, especially in the summer.

**General location:** The town of Newburyport, 35 miles north of Boston on the North Shore.

**Elevation change:** The terrain is relatively flat, with regular short climbs and descents.

**Seasons:** This can be a year-round ride. If you use the trails in the winter, though, avoid damaging cross-country ski tracks and avoid using muddy trails in any season.

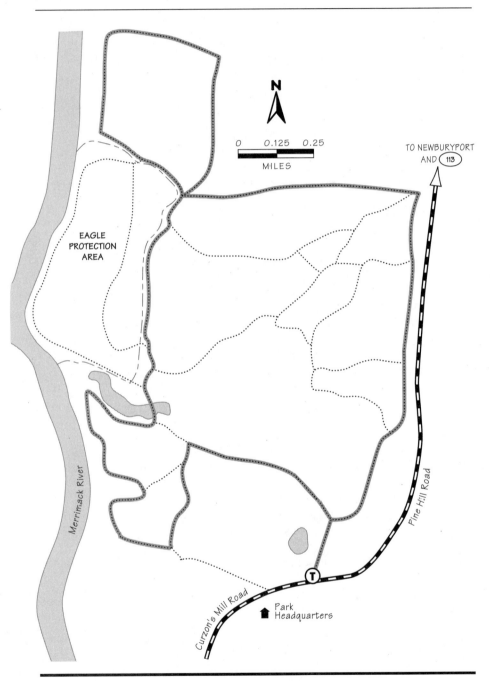

N

0    0.125    0.25

MILES

TO NEWBURYPORT
AND 113

EAGLE
PROTECTION
AREA

Merrimack River

Pine Hill Road

Curzon's Mill Road

T

Park
Headquarters

**Services:** All services are available in Newburyport.

**Hazards:** Watch for pedestrians and horseback riders, especially around blind corners. This park is a popular place for walking.

**Rescue index:** At most you will be about 0.25 mile from assistance.

**Land status:** Trails in a state park. To avoid accidents and also ensure that biking is always allowed here, be sure to yield to equestrians and avoid startling walkers.

**Maps:** Maps are stocked at the parking area. They include information about the site's history and flora.

**Finding the trail:** On Interstate 95 take Exit 57 for Newburyport, and turn right onto Massachusetts Highway 113. After 0.4 mile, turn left (at a cemetery) onto Noble Street. At the end of the street, turn left onto Ferry Road and follow the signs for the park. You will reach a parking area on the left after 1.4 miles.

**Sources of additional information:** Maudslay State Park (see Appendix).

**Notes on the trail:** Begin riding at a trailhead across from the parking area. To do a perimeter counterclockwise loop, fork right at the trailhead, cutting diagonally across the field northward. Stay on the carriage roads; do not cross open fields or use footpaths. Keep veering right along the boundary of the park. You will reach a four-way intersection of trails. Take a hard right. Continue riding until you approach the northeast border of the park, turn left, and you will reach the river.

Ride west along this scenic trail. There is also a side-trail loop to the right, through a low-lying, overgrown area. (From November 1 to March 31, a stretch of land along the river is fenced off. It is one of the few winter roosting areas in the Northeast for bald eagles. A trail skirts the area.)

When you reach the western edge of the park, turn south, and you will come back to the trailhead. To extend this ride, head toward the river again on another trail, exploring other loops.

# RIDE 25 *GEORGETOWN-ROWLEY STATE FOREST*

This moderate-to-easy 5-mile loop ride in a 1,000-acre forest alternates between single- and double-track trails and jeep roads. The route runs through deep woods past pine and oak trees, wetlands, and, at the northern edge of the forest, an active horse farm. This ride can be linked with more trails in two adjoining state parks to the southeast, Willowdale and Bradley Palmer (see Ride 26).

Throughout these woods you pass well-preserved stone walls. Local historians still debate exactly why European settlers built so many of them. They do know that many New England forests like this one were once farmland—before settlers discovered fishing and trading, and then the rockless Midwest. So they left their farms, which reverted to woods—except for hundreds of miles of impressive walls made of stacked field stones.

**General location:** The towns of Georgetown and Rowley, about 30 miles north of Boston.

**Elevation change:** The terrain is relatively flat, with a few short steep climbs and descents.

**Seasons:** Any time between late spring and late fall is good. Depending on the amount of rainfall, some low-lying trails can be muddy, especially in the spring.

**Services:** All services are available in Georgetown and other nearby towns, including Two For the Road, a bike shop on Main Street (Massachusetts Highway 113) in Georgetown and Cycle Stop on Union Street in Lawrence.

**Hazards:** Some of the trails and old roads in this forest are occasionally used by motorized off-road vehicles and horseback riders.

**Rescue index:** At most you can be about 1 mile from assistance.

**Land status:** State forest trails and roads.

**Maps:** Maps of several state forests in this part of Massachusetts are available at the headquarters of Bradley Palmer State Park on Asbury Street in Topsfield (see Ride 26).

**Finding the trail:** Take Exit 53 on Interstate 95 onto MA 97 west. After 1.5 miles, turn right onto Pingree Farm Road and take it to the trailhead.

**Notes on the trail:** From the parking area, take the trail on the right, which goes uphill. (The trail on the left heads east toward a bridge over I-95 and into the eastern half of the forest, with more trails.) Almost immediately, turn right onto a single-track trail that rolls up and down. Veer left and, after about 1 mile, you will reach a T junction with a wider trail. Turn left on it and soon

# RIDE 25 *GEORGETOWN-ROWLEY STATE FOREST*

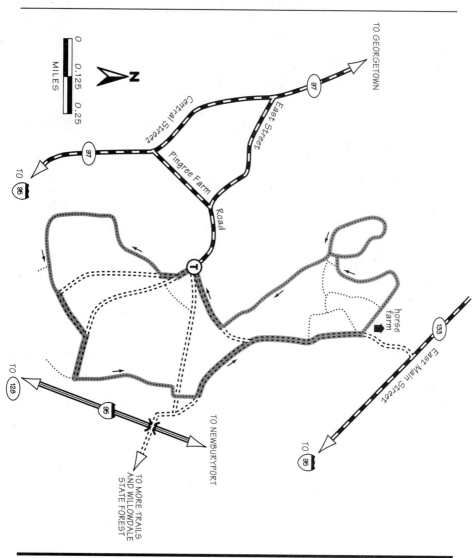

reach another T junction. Turn right on this looser, wider trail.

Just before reaching the highway, turn left sharply onto a single-track trail heading uphill. Veer left on this trail and reach a dirt road with a stone wall on the other side. Turn right onto the woods road, and soon left onto a narrower trail that heads north. (If you miss this turnoff, you will soon reach a bridge

Snaking stone walls are the remains of farmland in nineteenth-century New England. Georgetown, Massachusetts.

over the highway. This bridge hooks up with more trails, including those in Willowdale State Forest—see Ride 26.)

At the next junction, turn left onto a wider trail. Then fork right onto the wider trail. After about 0.2 mile, fork left onto a narrower trail. Take a right fork, rejoin the wider trail, and turn left just before reaching houses and a field. Ride along this horse farm, following a curving trail, veering right at a fork; just before a hill, turn right. Keep veering left around this enclosed loop. Just before going downhill, turn right onto a single-track trail. At a T junction turn right, and soon turn right again, reaching the trailhead.

# RIDE 26 *BRADLEY PALMER STATE PARK*

At the heart of the region north of Boston lies well-maintained Bradley Palmer State Park, a 720-acre former estate, offering around 10 miles of jeep roads and single-track trails winding through woods and open fields and along a river. Adjoining the park is the 2,400-acre Willowdale State Forest, with many more secluded dirt roads and double-track trails. The Bradley Palmer park headquarters is stocked with maps of several nearby state forests, including Willowdale.

There's riding in Bradley Palmer to satisfy all abilities—from wider, smoother dirt roads looping around the perimeter, to steeper, sometimes eroded trails rising and descending on two hills and along a river.

Although the trails are unmarked, the park is fairly compact and several distinctive areas help you stay oriented: large, grassy fields along the eastern border, paved Park Road, and the Ipswich River. Willowdale State Forest is three times larger and more difficult to navigate.

Even beginners should try the short climbs in Bradley Palmer to Moon Hill or Blueberry Hill, which are large, tranquil, mounded fields. Look for rose and rhododendron bushes along some paths—evidence of the park's past as the estate of businessman and benefactor Bradley Palmer.

If you're visiting this part of Massachusetts for the first time, you might also explore its nearby scenic coastline, with beaches, wildlife preserves, road-riding, and the annual 10-day Topsfield Fair held in the autumn.

**General location:** Topsfield, about 35 miles north of Boston.

**Elevation change:** This is rolling terrain, with many flat stretches and some short, steep climbs to two hills.

**Seasons:** Summer and fall are best for riding here.

**Services:** There are restrooms at the park headquarters and picnicking

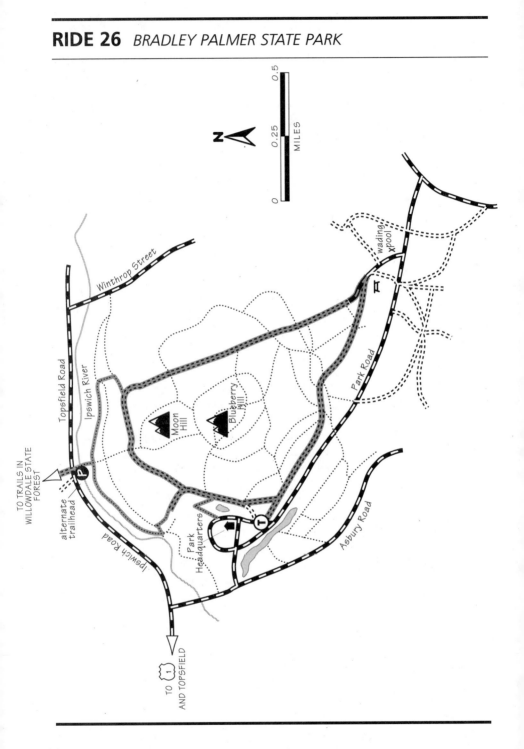

MILES

0  0.25  0.5

N

Winthrop Street

wading pool

Park Road

Topsfield Road

Ipswich River

Moon Hill

Blueberry Hill

TO TRAILS IN WILLOWDALE STATE FOREST

alternate trailhead

P

Ipswich Road

Park Headquarters

T

Asbury Road

TO 1 AND TOPSFIELD

Leafy seclusion. Bradley Palmer State Park, Topsfield, Massachusetts.

facilities. All other services are located along U.S. Highway 1 and in the towns of Topsfield, Hamilton, and Ipswich.

**Hazards:** This park is also used by horseback riders. When passing a horse, make sure to slow down and communicate with the rider, since some horses can become skittish around bicyclists. These trails are also used by hikers, and there is motorized traffic on paved Park Road. A few of the steeper trails in Bradley Palmer are quite eroded, so know your limits.

**Rescue index:** You will be no more than a half mile from a traveled road in Bradley Palmer State Park. However, in Willowdale State Forest you can be 1 mile from assistance.

**Land status:** Trails and roads in a public park and forest.

**Maps:** Trail maps of several state forests and parks in this area are stocked at the well-maintained headquarters near the parking lot.

**Finding the trail:** On Interstate 95, take Exit 50 onto US 1 north, toward Topsfield. After 2.5 miles you'll pass the Topsfield Fairground. At 4 miles, watch for signs for the state park, and turn right at a traffic light onto Ipswich Road. After 1.2 miles, turn right onto Asbury Road, and after 0.2 mile turn left into the state park (between tall stone pillars). Follow the signs to either the parking lot or the headquarters (to pick up a map). There's a pull-off parking area for Willowdale State Forest just 0.6 mile past Asbury Road on Ipswich Road.

**Sources of additional information:** Bradley Palmer State Park (see Appendix).

**Notes on the trail:** There are several choices for beginning a ride. Take a dirt road heading southeast out of the parking area (near paved Park Road) to reach either trails heading up two hills or the wide jeep roads circumventing the park. A jeep road eventually reaches a picnic and pool area on the other side of the park; it then veers northward, passing through several large fields, back to the main parking area. Crossing Park Road, one can take several trails along the southern edge of the park; they can be wetter and muddier under some conditions.

From the parking lot, you can also head behind the headquarters building and pick up the Nature Trail. This root-covered single-track trail connects up with the River Trail, which rolls along the scenic Ipswich River and further onto Essex County Greenbelt Association land. Then loop back on the dirt roads and trails on the east side of the park.

Halfway along the River Trail, you intersect a trail that crosses the Ipswich River on a wooden bridge. This trail will connect up with dirt roads on the other side of Ipswich Road in Willowdale State Forest. At a trailhead into the forest—just across Ipswich Road from the bridge—there's a sign indicating two blazed loops in the forest, red and blue. Willowdale has an extensive, interconnecting network of jeep roads and double-track trails. You can pick up a trail map of the forest at the Bradley Palmer headquarters.

# RIDE 27 *DOGTOWN*

This unusual habitat in the middle of Cape Ann on the North Shore, 30 miles away from Boston, is a popular site for both mountain biking and hiking. You can make all kinds of loops on the loose-gravel jeep roads, grassy double-track trails, and rocky single-track trails.

Once a colonial English settlement, Dogtown is now a secluded habitat with a varied landscape—highland woods with small trees, a marshy wetland fed by streams, an otherworldly habitat of white beech trees, a pine forest, and a reservoir with a narrow, old asphalt road circumventing it. There's also a small stone dam, built during the 1930s, which you can ride across on the Luce Trail. Also, several large "erratics"—boulders deposited by the retreating glaciers 10,000 years ago—dot the area, including Peter's Pulpit and The Whale's Jaw.

But these natural wonders are sometimes overshadowed by Dogtown's other famous rocks—several dozen modest-sized boulders with homilies carved into them, found on the Babson Boulder Trail. A century after the English colonized this area, which lies a few miles inland from the ocean, they decided that fishing and trading were easier than farming rock-strewn soil. So they moved back to the coast—and the town literally went to the dogs. By the 1930s, it was inhabited by social outcasts and wild canines.

Enter local financier and philanthropist Roger Babson, famous for predicting the stock market crash in 1929. He hired local stonecutters to carve inspirational sayings into the boulders in the area. It's hard to imagine what the down-and-out denizens of these woods thought about the rocks crying out, "Get a Job," "Never Try Never Win," "Courage," "Spiritual Power," "Help Mother," "Ideas," and a dozen other exhortations. As one local naturalist has written, "These carvings give you an idea of what Easter Island would look like if it had been settled by Calvinists." About 40 numerals carved into smaller rocks along dirt roads in Dogtown refer to historic sites that you can look up in the Gloucester Public Library.

Dogtown is located on Cape Ann, a summer vacation area that includes the seacoast towns of Rockport and Gloucester, and several dune-covered public beaches that fill up fast on summer weekends (although the water is cold). Just south of Gloucester lies Ravenswood Park, a small wooded area with trails.

**General location:** The towns of Gloucester and Rockport, 30 miles north of Boston.

**Elevation change:** The terrain is rolling, with regular short climbs and descents.

**Seasons:** Summer and fall are best for riding here; good drainage makes this a good spring ride, too.

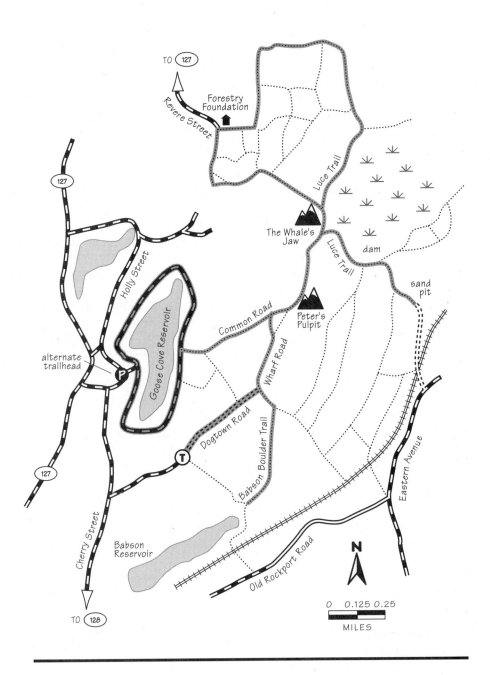

TO 127

Forestry
Foundation

Revere Street

127

Holly Street

Luce Trail

The Whale's
Jaw

Luce Trail

dam

sand
pit

Common Road

Peter's
Pulpit

Wharf Road

alternate
trailhead

P

Goose Cove Reservoir

Dogtown Road

T

Babson Boulder Trail

Eastern Avenue

127

Cherry Street

Babson
Reservoir

Old Rockport Road

N

TO 128

0    0.125 0.25
MILES

An urging from the past. Dogtown, Gloucester, Massachusetts.

**Services:** All services are available in Gloucester.

**Hazards:** Several of the single-track trails on the eastern side of Dogtown (east of Peter's Pulpit) are covered with rocks, making them barely passable.

**Rescue index:** At most you will be about 1 mile from assistance.

**Land status:** Abandoned old town roads and trails.

**Maps:** A trail map is available from the Gloucester Chamber of Commerce, open weekdays 8 A.M. to 5 P.M.

**Finding the trail:** On Massachusetts Highway 128, cross the Cape Ann Canal, and go around a rotary onto Massachusetts Highway 127. Immediately turn right onto Poplar Street and soon left onto Cherry Street. After less than a mile, you will pass a sign on the right for the Cape Ann Sportsmen's Club. A few hundred yards farther, turn right up a patchy old asphalt road. You will reach a parking area.

**Sources of additional information:** Local mountain bikers often congregate in the parking lot. *The Wilds of Cape Ann,* by Eleanor Pope, is a guide to the natural areas of Essex, Gloucester, and Rockport, and has information about this historical area.

**Notes on the trail:** As the map shows, there are a half-dozen different areas to explore in this lightly wooded area. Take the loose-gravel road that climbs out of the parking area (Dogtown Road). Turn right to check out Babson's boulders. Otherwise, fork left onto a single-track trail (Wharf Road), which leads to a jeep road (Common Road). For a descending sidetrip to the reservoir, turn left. It's a rolling 2-mile ride on an old asphalt road around the reservoir. Then double back on Common Road.

Turning right onto Common Road, you will pass a large boulder (Peter's Pulpit) on the right, and after about a half mile, watch for a left fork onto a narrower double-track trail. Forking there, you will reach The Whale's Jaw, a huge boulder in a small clearing (with a marker near it indicating "North"). This is a congregating spot for both hikers and cyclists.

To do a clockwise loop through a pine forest to the north—managed by the New England Forestry Foundation—ride around the boulder and pick up a single-track trail on the other side. Turn left at a T junction. Just before a stone wall appears on the right, turn right onto a single-track trail to enter the pine forest. (If you miss the turnoff, you'll soon reach a paved road.) Eventually you reach the foundation headquarters on Revere Street. To complete a loop through the forest, loop around back toward The Whale's Jaw from the other direction.

Finally, you can take Common Road to the Luce Trail, which leads to an attractive beech forest, with several rocky single-track trails off to the right. It's also possible to continue on the Luce Trail until it reaches an active sand pit. Go around the right side of the pit, turn right onto paved Eastern Avenue, then fork right onto Old Rockport Road, a gated two-wheel-drive dirt road. At the end of this road, turn right into the woods, cross the railroad tracks, and go around the right side of Babson Reservoir. Look for a trail climbing into the woods at the end of the reservoir. You should begin seeing boulders with sayings carved into them—you're now on Babson Boulder Trail. It comes out on the Moraine Trail. Turn left and reach Dogtown Road on the left.

# RIDE 28  *WRENTHAM STATE FOREST*

Often overshadowed by its better-known neighbor, F. Gilbert Hills ("Foxboro") State Forest (Ride 29), convenient Wrentham State Forest has miles of single- and double-track trails. Be prepared for some challenging riding here, too, since many of the trails roll and wind steeply over loose rock. It's also easy to become disoriented at times, since this elaborate network of trails is unmarked and often intricate.

A local mountain biking guru, known familiarly as The Old Coot, describes the forest this way: "How many singletracks would you say were too many? Now you can find out. The [forest] is laced with an almost uncountable number of motorcycle trails, jeep trails, old logging roads, and a few slightly maintained forest service roads. It does not have a campground, lake, river, or even a headquarters building—just 1,064 acres of well-drained, lightly hilled woodland trails. . . . The DEM [the State Department of Environmental Management] map does not show 90 percent of the existing trails . . . This means that you will have a great time getting yourself lost and found while you explore." Fortunately, the forest is bounded by four paved roads: Interstate 495, Taunton Street, Massachusetts Highway 140, and Madison Street.

The Civilian Conservation Corps (CCC) built many of the "roads" through this wooded landscape during the Great Depression era—as they did in so many public forests in Massachusetts. In 1936 and 1937, workers lived in camps in Wrentham Forest, planting trees and shrubs, clearing views, fighting fires, and creating roads and trails—for $1 a day.

Nowadays mountain bikers share the trails with cross-country skiers, snowmobilers, hikers, and the occasional motorized off-road vehicle. (On a Saturday afternoon, you might encounter a half-dozen motorized dirt bikes.) The famous Warner Trail, a hiking trail crossing Massachusetts from south to north, also runs through the forest; it's marked with white signs.

The forest landscape is a lively mix of red pine, Norway spruce, and many hardwood trees—oak, birch, beech, maple, ash, tupelo, and sassafras. If you missed the splendor of the fall foliage in places like Vermont and New Hampshire in early October, just take a trip to this forest in late October. At your feet, there's an understory of blueberry bushes (for snacking in July), alder, and witch hazel, as well as many large granite outcroppings. And if you're quiet, you might encounter some of the forest's feathered inhabitants: songbirds, quail, pheasant, turkeys, and hawks.

**General location:** Just south of the town of Wrentham, about 30 miles southwest of Boston. The forest is located just a mile from I-495 and four miles from I-95.

**Elevation change:** Rolling terrain, with many short, steep climbs and descents.

**Seasons:** This can be a four-season ride.

**Services:** The forest has no amenities—just woods and trails. All services are available in the towns of Wrentham and Foxboro, and along U.S. Highway 1.

**Hazards:** Some trails have loose scrabble and an occasional low sandy area, requiring bike-handling skills, especially on descents. Also, be prepared to be disoriented for brief periods of time, since the trails in this relatively compact area are unmarked and sometimes intricate. (A compass will help you stay oriented.) The trails are closed on Saturdays during deer-hunting season in the fall—check with the rangers about the dates. Hunting is not allowed on Sundays.

**Rescue index:** You can be about a half mile from a well-traveled road.

# RIDE 28 *WRENTHAM STATE FOREST*

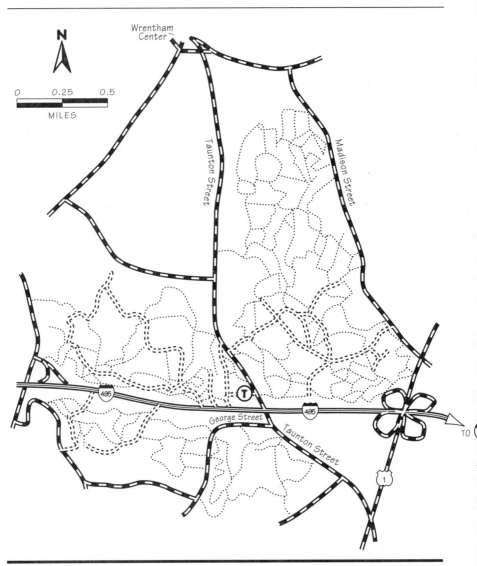

**Land status:** Trails and roads in a public forest.

**Maps:** There is a large trail map on a board at the parking area. You can request a map from the Department of Environmental Management (see Appendix). Many of the narrower trails in this forest are unmapped.

**Finding the trail:** On I-495 take Exit 14B onto US 1 south. After 0.6 mile, at a stoplight, turn right sharply onto Taunton Street. After another 0.6 mile, just after crossing a bridge over I-495, turn left into a small gravel parking lot at a brown state forest sign on the right.

**Sources of additional information:** Wrentham State Forest (see Appendix).

**Notes on the trail:** As this map shows, the entire forest is divided into three sections by two paved roads: Taunton Street and I-495. (Remember, the trails were here first—it's the highways that intrude.) To reach the larger eastern portion, which has the most trails and the deepest, quietest woods, you can either take a single-track trail heading north out of the parking area, turn right at the first four-way intersection in the woods, and cross Taunton Street, picking up a jeep road at a large gate on the other side—or ride north on Taunton Street for a short distance and turn right onto the same jeep road at the gate.

If it is your first time riding here, you might begin on the fire roads heading east-west in the southern part of the forest and on the trails along a fence near I-495. Also, there's a marked loop winding through the southern part of this section, the blue-blazed Acorn Trail. To the north, the trails quickly become more convoluted. (As one local rider says, "Will you get lost here? Sure—but you're in a box.")

From the parking area, you can also head through a gate onto a double-track trail that descends into the northwestern part of the forest. There you can pick up several jeep roads. Or begin at a trailhead off George Street to explore the smaller southwest section of the forest.

---

# RIDE 29 F. GILBERT HILLS STATE FOREST

---

This area, commonly known as "Foxboro" state forest, boasts one of the most extensive networks of single-track trails and woods roads in southeastern Massachusetts. The ride in this book is a challenging 10-mile loop, created in 1992, most of which uses single-track trails winding through secluded woods, crisscrossing other trails and gravel roads. To do a shorter ride, you can take the woods roads that intersect the loop (two come at about 5 and 7 miles).

This 1,025-acre forest (it seems larger) is undeveloped—no two-wheel-drive roads, swimming areas, or camping. Instead, it's a habitat of light woods dotted with granite boulders, a few picnic tables at the trailhead, and a complex network of trails for hiking, biking, and horseback riding. The gravelly terrain on many of the jeep roads is glacial till, left behind when the glaciers melted and withdrew northward 15,000 years ago.

Nearby Wrentham State Forest is another favorite local mountain biking area (Ride 28).

**General location:** The town of Foxboro, 35 miles southwest of Boston.

**Elevation change:** Although the terrain here is relatively flat, there are many regular short climbs and descents.

**Seasons:** These (mostly) well-drained trails and gravel roads provide good conditions for riding in otherwise wetter conditions, such as in the spring. Summer offers shade and autumn brings colorful foliage.

**Services:** There is a water spigot at the fire station at the headquarters. All other services are in Foxboro.

**Hazards:** Some of the single-track trails can be difficult—less-experienced riders should dismount and walk down eroded stretches. Although one can get disoriented in this network of trails, the area is bounded by paved roads. As always, watch out for other trail users.

**Rescue index:** You will be about 1.5 miles from assistance.

**Land status:** State forest roads and trails.

**Maps:** Maps should be stocked at the main parking lot next to a large trail map on a board. Otherwise, contact the Department of Environmental Management (see Appendix).

**Finding the trail:** Take Exit 8 on U.S. Highway 95, and bear right toward Foxboro on Mechanic Street. When you reach the commons in Foxboro, go around it and out the other side onto South Street. After 1.3 miles, turn right onto Mill Street, then veer left, following the brown state forest signs. After 0.3 mile, you will reach the forest parking lots on the right and left. Park in the left-hand lot, which is not gated at dusk.

**Sources of additional information:** F. Gilbert Hills State Forest (see Appendix).

**Notes on the trail:** This 10-mile loop is marked by green triangular mountain-bike signs on trees at many intersections. You must remember to look for these signs. Sometimes you will be turning off a wider trail onto a narrower one. If you don't see a green mountain-bike sign for a while, turn around and find the last one. The trails on the back side of this loop (the most challenging ones) are also marked by yellow all-terrain-vehicle signs. At several points, you can bail out on a gravel road heading back to the parking area.

Head uphill into the woods on a wide path next to the map board at the parking lot. Within a few hundred yards, fork right. (This ride comes out on the left-hand fork.) When you reach a T junction, after less than a half mile, turn left, fork left at the next turn, and you will reach paved Granite Street. Directly across the road, pick up the trail, which veers left, crosses the paved road again, and heads onto a dirt woods road, High Rock Road. (You can do a short loop now by making left turns on all the dirt roads.)

Cleaning up and clearing out. KRISTINA HOLLY PHOTO

A few hundred feet along the woods road, turn right onto a single-track trail that heads north. You will reach unpaved Messenger Road. Turn right here, and take the first left fork onto another dirt road. Fork left onto the next uphill trail and head north on the left side of Upper Dam Pond, following the trail as it veers south. Just before you reach Messenger Road again, look for a green mountain-bike sign on a trail on the right. Keep following the green signs. You can shorten this ride by turning southeast on an intersecting dirt road.

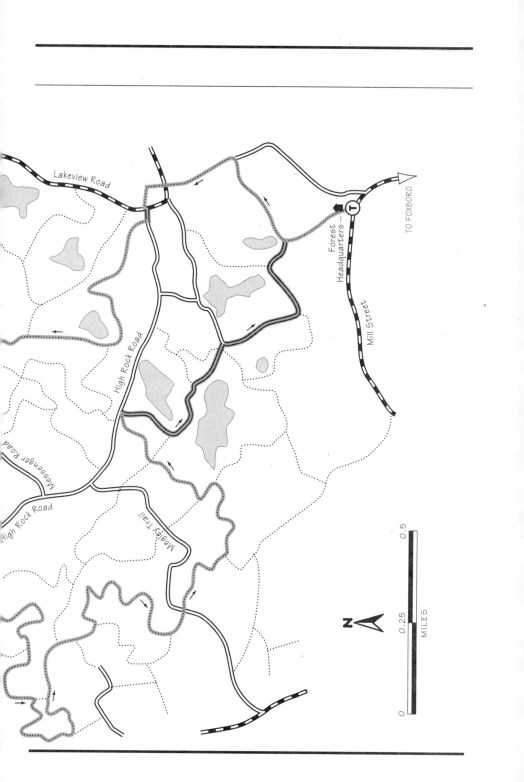

# RIDE 30 *AMES NOWELL STATE PARK*

This 5-mile loop links a host of single-track trails and two power-line trails in this sunny, wooded park. The riding conditions vary widely, from fairly easy to somewhat difficult. You begin by paralleling a large pond—but avoid the trail skirting the shoreline. After cruising on a paved rural road for a half mile, the ride explores a power-line trail lined with light vegetation for a short distance, before picking up a network of single-track trails. Finally, it's cruising on a double-track trail back to the trailhead and picnic area. Along the way, you will cross a wetland and several small streams.

More trails connect up with this loop, including a mostly rideable north-south powerline running from Braintree to Plymouth.

**General location:** The town of Abington, just off MA 24 and MA 3, 20 miles south of Boston.

**Elevation change:** There are a few short climbs and descents on this ride.

**Seasons:** Any time between late spring and late fall is good. Expect some muddy areas in the spring and after a rainfall in any season.

**Services:** All services are available along MA 18 and in the towns of Abington and Brockton.

**Hazards:** Watch for occasional obstructions on the more secluded trails.

**Rescue index:** At most you can be about 1 mile from a traveled road.

**Land status:** State park trails, a town road, and a powerline with a public trail.

**Maps:** There may be maps available at the entrance, or contact the Department of Environmental Management (see Appendix).

**Finding the trail:** From MA 3, south of Boston, take Exit 16B onto MA 18 south toward Abington. After about 5 miles, turn right onto MA 123 toward Brockton. After 0.8 mile, fork right onto Groveland Street, then after 1 mile, turn right onto Linwood Street. You will reach a pair of stone gates at the park entrance. The main parking lot closes at 4 P.M. Park outside the gates if you plan to stay longer.

**Sources of additional information:** Ames Nowell State Park (see Appendix).

**Notes on the trail:** Biking is allowed on all the trails and roads in this park, except for Trail 2, which skirts the eastern shoreline of Cleveland Pond. Although there are plenty of turns on this ride, you can't get too lost since the area is compact, bounded on all sides by paved roads, and intersected by two distinct powerlines.

Here's a turn-by-turn description of a 5-mile loop: Pass through the large gate on the left side of the parking lot and onto a narrow paved road. (Watch

# RIDE 30 *AMES NOWELL STATE PARK*

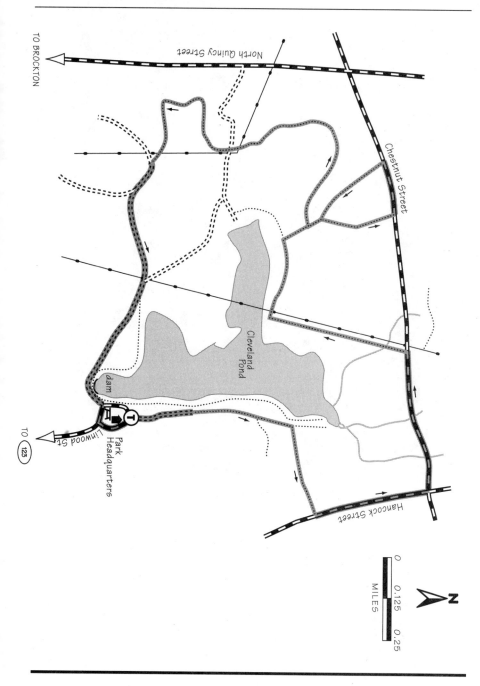

Single-track solitude. Ames Nowell State Park, Abington,
Massachusetts.

for other park users in this area.) Almost immediately, fork right onto an
unpaved jeep road.

After about a half mile, just before you reach the pond, turn right onto a
single-track trail. You will come out on paved Hancock Street. Turn left on it
and left again at Chestnut Street, the first major intersection. After about a
half mile, watch for a gated double-track trail on the left at a powerline. Turn
left onto the power-line trail and, after about a half mile, turn right just before
the pond.

After another few tenths of a mile, veer right on the wider trail, and, after another 0.1 mile, turn off this wider trail onto a single-track trail. (You can also follow the wider trail to Chestnut Street. Turn left, and after 0.3 mile pick up another trail on the left. Veer right on it, and return to the same spot.) Follow the single-track trail as it winds around in the woods and comes out on a second powerline. Turn left on the powerline, and after another 0.2 mile, turn right off it, then right almost immediately.

You now will wind around another single-track trail (once a moto-cross trail) and pick up the same powerline. Turn right on the powerline, turn left at a junction with a dirt road. Stay on the dirt road (now heading east), and you will cross the first powerline. You can then take the dirt road all the way back to the parking area, or fork left off it onto a single-track trail that runs next to the pond. You will come out at a dam at the pond; cross it and reach the parking area.

# RIDE 31 *WOMPATUCK STATE PARK*

This moderate 8-mile ride circumscribes the western half of a 3,500-acre "park," with about 30 miles of trails and old roads, as well as a 12-mile paved bike path—all within 20 miles of Boston.

After riding southward on single- and double-track trails, you can loop back on the same trails, or cross over to the eastern side of the park and explore several newly built single-track trails (as yet unmapped), as well as the winding, paved bike path.

This large, accessible park also attracts road cyclists, cross-country skiers, hikers, and campers (400 campsites) to its wooded landscape of oaks and evergreens, old stone walls, ponds, and a popular fresh-water spring.

Just east of the park, a trail links up with more trails and unpaved roads in Whitney and Thayer Woods, managed by the Trustees of Reservations, a private organization.

You might also want to check out the nearby seacoast towns of Hingham, Cohasset, and Scituate, with their public beaches and some of the most scenic road-riding anywhere. Another Trustees of Reservations property is nearby World's End (off Massachusetts Highway 3A near Nantasket Beach), with gentle, unpaved roads for biking.

**General location:** The towns of Hingham and Cohasset, about 20 miles south of Boston.

**Elevation change:** This ride gains about 150 feet, with an optional climb of another 100 feet.

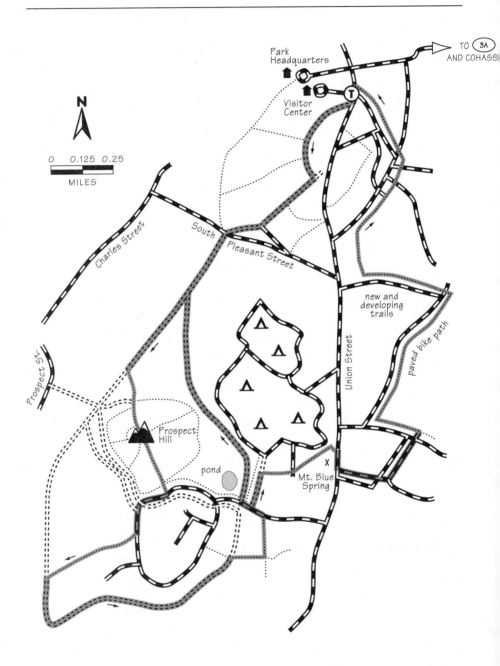

Trailbuilding. KRISTINA HOLLY PHOTO

**Seasons:** Any time between late spring and late fall. Avoid riding on the trails in wet conditions.

**Services:** Water is found at Mt. Blue Spring, halfway along the ride on paved Union Street. Restrooms are at the southern side of the campground (400 sites, with showers, April 15 through October 15.) All other services are available along MA 228 and in nearby towns.

**Hazards:** Watch for minor obstructions on the trails and the occasional horseback rider. There may be mosquitoes in low-lying areas in the spring and early summer.

**Rescue index:** At most you can be about 1 mile from assistance.

**Land status:** State park trails and roads.

**Maps:** Maps are available at the visitor center, across from the trailhead.

**Finding the trail:** On MA 3 south, take Exit 14 onto MA 228 north toward Hingham. After about 4 miles, watch for a brown sign for the state park. Turn right just before a handsome white church on the right. After 0.8 mile, you will reach the park entrance.

**Sources of additional information:** Wompatuck State Park (see Appendix).

**Notes on the trail:** This popular riding site in the Greater Boston area has expanded its trail network in the past several years. The 8-mile ride on this map is one possible loop through its western section. The abundance of different routes in this 3,500-acre park—single-track trails, double-track trails, and jeep roads—can confuse the first-time rider. It's one reason group rides often congregate in the parking lot at the visitor center on both weekends and weekday evenings.

If you're exploring the park on your own, you might want to bring a compass (always a good idea) to stay oriented. Try cruising through the park first on the wider trails and paved roads, to familiarize yourself with various trailheads and features—such as the camping area, asphalt loop roads, Union Street, and the paved bike path—before exploring the more wooded and secluded trails.

# RIDE 32 *MASSASOIT STATE PARK*

Not as well-known to mountain bikers as some neighboring state parks—like Freetown and Myles Standish—Massasoit deserves to be. Located at the junction of coastal and inland habitats, this 1,500-acre area is laced with 10 to 15 miles of single-track trails and several miles of woods roads, weaving through a lightly wooded landscape. Most of the riding here is moderate, with a few more technical climbs on steeper trails and easier riding on the flat, wide roads.

Quite a few trails in the park aren't mapped—but the area is relatively compact, so exploring them without getting lost is possible. In particular, don't miss the networks of trails north of Lake Rico, which roll through the woods before coming out at the shoreline, with mid-range views.

Massasoit may not be as prominent as some other parks in southeastern Massachusetts among cyclists—but it's a favorite among campers. In fact, all of its 120 campsites can fill up on an August weekend.

The name "Massasoit" has a meaning for the local Wompanoag tribe that's similar to "Washington" for European Americans. Chief Massasoit governed what is now Massachusetts and Rhode Island in the early seventeenth century. In 1621, he signed the first peace treaty in New England with John Carver, governor of the Plymouth Colony. In gratitude, the Pilgrims invited Chief Massasoit and his tribe to a Thanksgiving dinner. Here's the entire treaty:

- That neither he [Chief Massasoit] nor any of his should injure or do hurt to any of our people.
- And if any of his did hurt to any of ours, he should send the offender, that we might punish him.
- That if any of our tools were taken away when our people were at work, he should cause them to be restored; and if ours did any harm to any of his, we would do the like to them.
- If any did unjustly war against him, we would aid him; if any did war against us, he should aid us.
- He should send to his neighbor confederates, to certify them of this, that they might not wrong us, but might be likewise comprised in the conditions of peace.
- That when their men came to us, they should leave their bows and arrows behind them, as we should do our pieces when we came to them.
- Lastly, that doing thus, King James would esteem of him as his friend and ally.

The treaty was never broken.

# RIDE 32 *MASSASOIT STATE PARK*

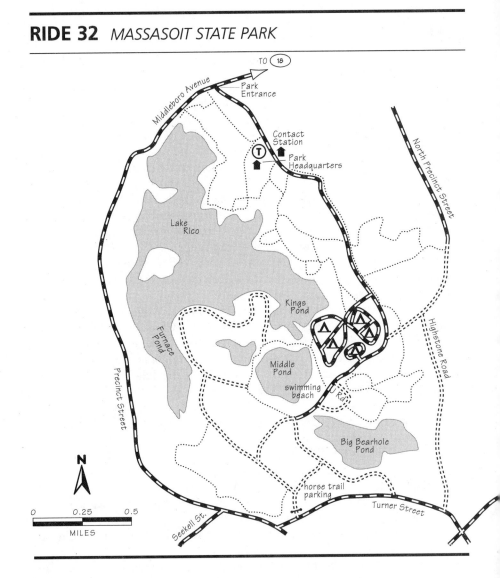

**General location:** The town of East Taunton, 20 miles west of Plymouth, Massachusetts, 25 miles east of Providence, Rhode Island, and 40 miles south of Boston, Massachusetts. The park is 2.5 miles from Interstate 495.

**Elevation change:** Most of the trails here are rolling, with some short, steep climbs (and descents). The woods roads are much flatter.

**Seasons:** This is a good three-season ride (summer, fall, and winter).

**Services:** The camping area has water, restrooms, and 120 camping sites.

Hard-packed sand trail. Massasoit State Park, East Taunton, Massachusetts.

There's also a swimming beach in the park. All other services are available along U.S. Highway 44 and in the towns of Middleboro and Taunton.

**Hazards:** Expect people, especially children, around the roads near the camping area. On the trails, watch for hikers, as well as the occasional stretch of loose rock or sandiness.

**Rescue index:** You will be no more than a one-quarter mile from a traveled road.

**Land status:** Trails and bridle paths in a state park.

**Maps:** Available in the contact station at the park entrance. *Note:* The state map does not show most of the single-track trails in the park.

**Finding the trail:** Take Exit 6 (Middleboro/Plymouth) off I-495 onto US 44. Turn east and you will reach a rotary in a half mile. (There's a Friendly's Restaurant at the rotary—a good place to rendezvous with others.) At the rotary, get onto Massachusetts Highway 18 south. After about a half mile, look for a right turn with signs: "East Taunton, 4 miles" and "Airport." Turn right, and after 2.2 miles, look for the low, large, brown park sign on the left. Turn in, and continue for a few hundred yards to a large parking lot on the right, just before the contact station. (There's a modest fee for all-day use of the beach and other park facilities.)

**Sources of additional information:** Massasoit State Park (see Appendix).

**Notes on the trail:** A convenient trailhead lies just behind the main parking area. Heading southwest, you can fork either northward or southward on a network of trails that's not entirely mapped, using Lake Rico as a natural border. To the south, after skirting the camping area, pick up the woods roads south of Lake Rico. In the southeastern part of the park (just above Big Blackhole Pond), there's another network of trails, which hooks up with a trail paralleling the paved road through the park, heading north back toward the parking area.

# RIDE 33 *MYLES STANDISH STATE FOREST*

This 16,000-acre forest is one of the largest pine barrens in the country. Pine barrens are aquifers—the purest known water is stored underneath their vast expanses of pines and oaks. (There's a spigot at the trailhead.) The challenging 7-mile loop ride here explores this unusual "minimalist" habitat of pine trees and relatively few other plant species. Among the forest's other features are 35 small ponds, called kettle ponds, formed when glaciers melted at the end of the Ice Age. In spring and fall, the forest is also a stopover for migrating birds.

The 30 or so miles of trails and unpaved roads here vary from hard-packed dirt to grass and loose sand. Some of the sandier terrain can be more difficult riding. In general, trails designated with red markers (bridle paths) are less sandy than some of the unpaved roads. There's also a 15-mile paved bike path that rolls up and down with the contours of the land.

Two of the ponds in the forest have swimming beaches. Just outside the forest you can also cruise on paved roads along cranberry bogs. This part of southeastern Massachusetts produces more cranberries than any other region in the world.

You might also visit Plymouth, 4 miles to the east. There you can tour Plimouth (original spelling) Plantation, a reconstructed Puritan village. The forest also lies 15 miles from the beginning of Cape Cod (at the Cape Cod Canal in Bourne).

Myles Standish, who was *not* a Pilgrim, arrived on the Mayflower and became the military leader of the Plymouth Colony.

**General location:** The towns of Plymouth and Carver, 45 miles south of Boston.

**Elevation change:** Overall, the terrain is flat, but with many short climbs and descents.

**Seasons:** You can ride in this area year-round. The sandy trails are well drained in the spring, and there is usually little snow in the winter. Although summer can be hot, you can cool off at the beaches.

**Services:** Water is available at the trailhead near the forest headquarters. A nearby bike shop is Martha's Cycle on Massachusetts Highway 3A in North Plymouth. The forest has several hundred campsites, open from mid-April to mid-October, with showers (no reservations necessary). There is also a grocery store with a deli a few miles from the trailhead toward South Carver.

**Hazards:** Although the trails and roads in this forest are distinct, they are also plentiful and often resemble each other. Carrying a map and compass is a good idea. Also, bring plenty of water on a longer ride, especially during the summer.

**Rescue index:** At most you will be several miles from assistance on secluded trails.

**Land status:** State forest trails and roads. Biking is not allowed along the shorelines of the ponds or in one area marked for hikers only or on the groomed cross-country ski trails during the winter.

**Maps:** Maps are available at the forest headquarters.

**Finding the trail:** From the north, take Exit 5 on MA 3. Turn right onto Long Pond Road and follow the brown state forest signs for about 3 miles, until you reach the paved access road on the right. This road runs diagonally through the forest for 5 miles; taking it is a good way to familiarize yourself with the

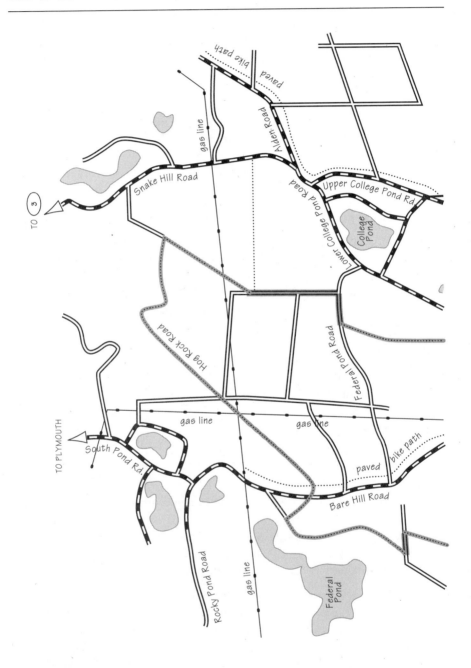

N

MILES
0    0.5    1

Upper College Pond Road

Lower College Pond Road

gas line

Bare Hill Road

Dunham Road

West Line Road

TO CARVER

Fearing Pond

swimming area

Charge Pond

swimming area

gas line

paved bike path

East Head Reservoir

drinking water

Forest Headquarters

paved bike path

Barrett Pond

T

Miles of secluded roads through a pine barren. Myles Standish State Forest, Plymouth, Massachusetts.

area and intersecting trailheads. Note the paved bike path on the left, which parallels the road.

From the west and south, take Exit 2 (South Carver) on Interstate 495. Follow MA 58 into South Carver, then brown signs into the forest.

**Sources of additional information:** Myles Standish State Forest (see Appendix).

**Notes on the trail:** There are dozens of options for riding in the forest; the map in this book shows one large loop through several sections. From the parking lot at the forest headquarters, take the paved bike path heading northwest, behind and to the left of the headquarters. You will cross a paved road. Turn left off the bike path at the first intersection with an unpaved, sandy jeep road

(Barrett Road). At a stop sign, turn left and almost immediately right into a parking area. Follow the ATV (all-terrain vehicle) signs at the other side of the parking lot onto a narrow double-track trail.

At a four-way intersection, get off this trail (which becomes eroded) and onto the dirt road heading in the same direction on the right. After about another half mile, you will reach an intersection with another ride jeep road, Dunham Road. Turn right on it, and ride for about 1.5 miles on this sandy, rolling road, crossing a couple of unpaved roads (which you can take to the right for a shorter ride), until you reach T junction with Federal Pond Road.

You can do a longer, more challenging loop by turning left onto Federal Pond Road, then right at the next junction onto West Line Road. Follow the yellow dirt-bike signs past Federal Pond on the left, and as you pass the pond, veer off the main road onto a narrower trail on the right. You will cross a paved road, the paved bike path (which you can take back to the trailhead), and a gas line. Now you're on a secluded trail on the northern edge of the forest, which winds southward, eventually reaching Federal Pond Road.

You now have three options for returning to the trailhead: jeep roads, narrower bridle paths, or the bike path. One way back is to turn right onto Federal Pond Road and pick up a bridle path on the left. This trail will reach a T junction with unpaved Three Cornered Pond Road. Turn left on it, and soon reach paved Lower College Pond Road. Turn right onto the pavement for a short distance, and pick up a trail on the other side going uphill to the right.

At the top of the hill, with a pond on the right, turn left onto a bridle path (red markers) named Negas Road. This trail will intersect the bike path just before reaching Upper College Pond Road. Turn right on the bike path and follow signs painted on it for the headquarters, or head southeast on the bike path toward Fearing Pond and Charge Pond.

The 15-mile bike path has three main sections: one heading northwest for 4 miles, one northeast for 5 miles, and several interconnecting loops to the south for 6 miles. The 4-mile out-and-back path heading northwest is more rolling and faster than the longer out-and-back ride to the northeast.

To do a 5-mile loop to the south, ride due east on the paved access road from the forest headquarters. The bike path comes up on the left at a brown gate. After less than a half mile, turn right at a fork in the path and then right again at the next fork.

After crossing two paved roads and a parking area, you will reach a T junction. Turn right to do a side trip to Charge Pond. Or turn left to continue on the loop. After about another 1.5 miles, you will reach another swimming pond, Fearing Pond. After passing that, white signs painted on the path at an intersection indicate several destinations: forest headquarters, Charge Pond, and Plymouth.

# RIDE 34 *FREETOWN STATE FOREST*

This 6,500-acre forest, a favorite mountain biking site in southeastern Massachusetts, has several dozen miles of trails and unpaved roads—including a challenging 20-mile single-track loop marked with yellow signs. The moderate 10-mile ride here connects double-track and single-track trails and dirt and gravel roads. At many junctions, though, you can take side trips to create either longer, more difficult rides or shorter, easier ones.

Exploring this forest will give you a taste of a coastal habitat, with its hard-packed, sandy ground and woodscape dominated by small pine and oak trees.

About halfway on the ride (at the junction of Copicut and Bell Rock roads), you will pass a sign indicating that this section is part of the Wompanoag Indian Reservation. Like most Native American tribes in the Northeast, the Wompanoags public hold powwows—with chanting, dancing, and crafts activities—at various times during the year.

**General location:** The towns of Freetown and Fall River.

**Elevation change:** This terrain is flat, except for regular short, steep hills on the single-track trails.

**Seasons:** This can be a four-season ride, if there is little snow and not too much rain in the spring.

**Services:** Restrooms and a drinking fountain are available near the parking lot. All other services are in Freetown and Fall River.

**Hazards:** Be prepared to switch riding techniques from the wide, smooth dirt roads to the rugged, narrower trails.

**Rescue index:** At most you will be about 1 mile from assistance on secluded trails.

**Land status:** Old roads and trails in a state forest. *Note:* The trails in the area southeast of Bell Rock and Copicut roads are on an Indian reservation—respect this land.

**Maps:** There is a large trail map on a board at the parking lot. You can send for a map from the Department of Environmental Management (see Appendix).

**Finding the trail:** Take Exit 10 on Massachusetts Highway 24 and turn right toward signs for Profile Rock and Freetown State Forest. After a half mile, turn left in Assonet at a sign for the state forest. Almost immediately, fork right at another forest sign. At 1.5 miles, you will pass Profile Rock on the left. At 2.5 miles, turn right at a brown sign for the forest, drive up the paved access road, and turn left into a large paved parking lot across from the headquarters.

**Sources of additional information:** Freetown State Forest (see Appendix).

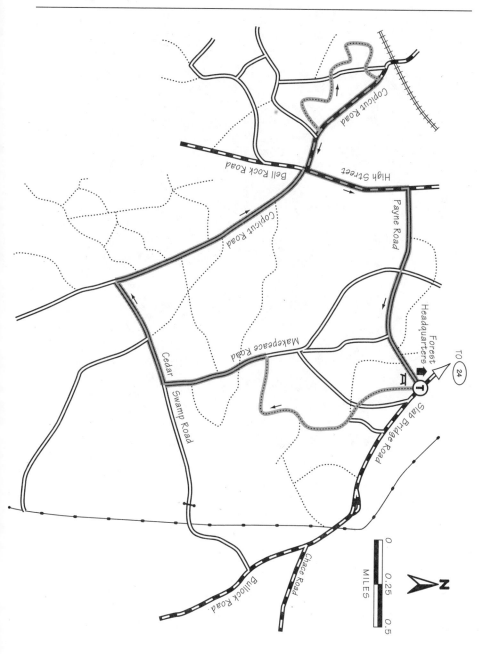

Log-hopping with room to spare. Freetown State Forest, Fall River, Massachusetts.

**Notes on the trail:** This ride has quite a few turns on it, since it explores several areas in the forest. For an easier ride, just stay on the dirt roads. For more difficult riding, take the marked single-track trails, mainly southwest of Copicut Road.

Ride past several picnic tables away from the parking lot and pick up a double-track trail heading southeast. Turn right at a T junction, fork left, and go straight through a four-way intersection. (For a more challenging ride, turn right at the four-way intersection and soon fork left onto a single-track trail, which rejoins this loop farther along.)

At the next T junction with a wide two-wheel-drive dirt road, Makepeace Road, turn left. Then turn right onto the next two-wheel-drive road, Cedar Swamp Road. Turn right at the next woods road, Copicut Road. (Or you can take a fairly easy single-track trail on the right side of Cedar Swamp Road that rejoins the loop on Copicut Road.) You will reach a paved four-way intersection. For a shorter ride, turn right onto High Street. For a longer ride, turn left onto Bell Rock Road.

Otherwise, head straight on Copicut Road, and look for the second left onto a single-track trail, then immediately veer right on it. Twist and turn on this single-track trail, cross a wide dirt road, and continue on the trail. Take the next right turn, go through an intersection, turn left at a T junction, and you will reach Copicut Road again. Turn right, then left onto paved High Street. Ride downhill and turn right at a forest sign onto unpaved Payne Road. For a longer, more difficult ride, turn left at the second metal gate on Payne Road, turn right several times, and rejoin either Payne Road or Makepeace Road. Otherwise, ride straight on Payne Road, fork left at a major intersection, and reach the parking lot.

# RIDE 35 *MASHPEE RIVER WOODLANDS*

If you're looking for some fun, stimulating, and easy single-track riding on Cape Cod, these 5 miles of rolling trails will fit the bill. Beginners will be moderately challenged by these winding, rolling paths, while more experienced riders should appreciate the tight turns and occasional log jumps. (For a longer ride, just do the trails in both directions.) And take some time to stop and appreciate the habitat.

Because this is scenic conservation land along a river, expect to meet occasional hikers—and slow down. As a conservation area, it's especially important that cyclists (like all users) stay on the trails and do not pick plants or disturb the habitat. Also, this area is part of an ongoing effort to create trail networks linking open spaces in all 15 towns on Cape Cod, from Falmouth to Provincetown.

This region is the home of the Wompanoag tribe. This Native American people still inhabit the Mashpee area, and you can find out more about them from the Wompanoag Tribal Council (see Appendix). There's also the Wompanoag Museum on Route 130 in Mashpee, with artifacts and information—and a bike path running past it (see Appendix). Another easy off-road ride on the Cape circumvents Nickerson State Park in Brewster, using around 7 miles of dirt roads and double-track trails. The park is also a popular camping area, with more than 400 sites.

# RIDE 35  *MASHPEE RIVER WOODLANDS*

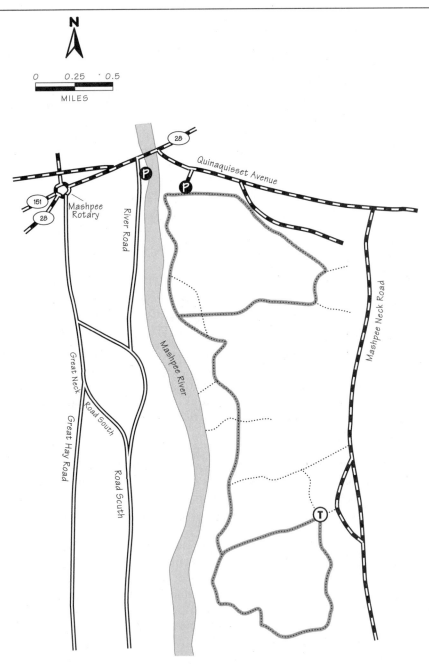

Winding, rolling singletrack. Mashpee River Woodlands, Mashpee, Massachusetts.

For more-challenging riding on the Cape, there's the Trail of Tears in Sandwich (Exit 4 on Massachusetts Highway 6, then right onto Chase Road), as well as other informal sites, which you can find out about by dropping in a local bike shop.

Or, for a change, pump up the tires and try the paved 20-mile-long Cape Cod Rail Trail, which runs from Dennis to Eastham.

**General location:** The town of Mashpee.

**Elevation change:** The overall terrain is flat, but the trails roll up and down.

**Seasons:** Any time between late spring and late fall. Avoid riding in wet conditions.

**Services:** All services are available in Mashpee and along MA 28. A nearby bike shop is Corner Cycle in Falmouth.

**Hazards:** Less-experienced riders should use caution around the tight curves on these trails to avoid unwanted encounters with trees. Also, watch for hikers, especially around blind corners. This is a conservation area, so be sure to ride respectfully and avoid leaving tire tracks.

**Rescue index:** You will be near well-traveled roads.

**Land status:** Trails in a public park.

**Maps:** A large trail map and a box of maps are at the trailhead. An excellent map and guide to history, features, and nature of the Mashpee River Woodlands is available from the Mashpee Conservation Office (see Appendix).

**Finding the trail:** Take U.S. Highway 6 across the Sagamore Bridge onto Cape Cod, and after 4 miles, take Exit 2 onto MA 130 south, toward Mashpee and Sandwich. After about 8.5 miles, turn right onto MA 28. Continue for just under 2 miles, and turn left sharply onto Quinaquisset Avenue, which is 0.3 mile east of the traffic circle in Mashpee. You will pass a sign on the right: "Mashpee River Woodlands/North Parking Lot." You can park there or continue on to Mashpee Neck Road, turning right, and watch for a parking area on the right at another sign: "Mashpee River Woodlands."

**Sources of additional information:** Mashpee Conservation Office (see Appendix).

**Notes on the trail:** You can explore this compact area in any direction you want. Getting lost is difficult. There are also several dirt roads on the other side of the river.

# RIDE 36 *MARTHA'S VINEYARD STATE PARK / TOUR I*

This 12-mile ride explores a large, sunny forest in the heart of Martha's Vineyard. In the summer, the forest is a calm "eye of the storm" on this bustling, popular vacation island just off Cape Cod. These 5,000-plus acres of pines, oaks, blueberry bushes, and low-lying groundcover are laced with about 40 miles of fire roads and double-track and single-track trails. It's a good place for novice riders, since it's flat and fairly smooth, as well as accomplished cyclists, who will find its long, rolling fire roads and trails fun.

Tour I is the easier of the two in this book—in length, difficulty, and complexity. It alternates between fire lanes, single-track and double-track trails, and a few stretches on a paved bike path. Almost all of the terrain is

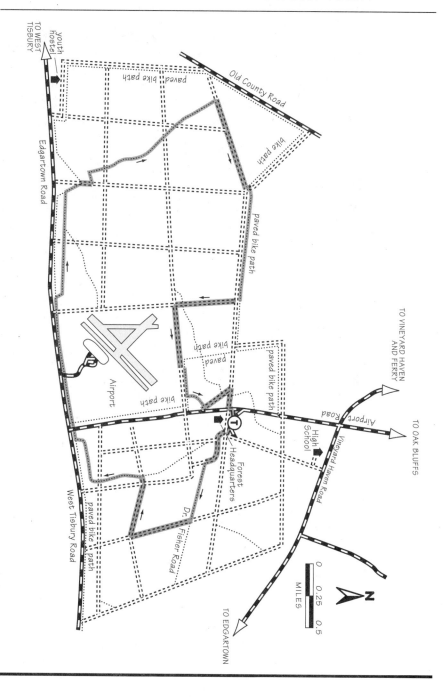

hard-packed sand. No motorized vehicles are allowed in the park, so it's a tranquil environment, where you might see birds and other wildlife, or meet up with hikers from a nearby youth hostel and occasional horseback riders.

The island also has 100 miles or more of off-road riding *outside* the state forest, using both single-track trails and jeep roads (see photo). Almost all towns on Martha's Vineyard—except for Aquinnah, formerly called Gay Head—have trails. Ask at a bike shop in a town (Cycle Works in Vineyard Haven is a good one) or a chamber of commerce. Some trails are on private land and rideable only in the winter. There are several good maps of the island.

**General location:** In the middle of Martha's Vineyard, 3.5 miles south of the ferry landing in the town of Vineyard Haven.

**Elevation change:** The terrain is flat, with occasional short dips and hills.

**Seasons:** This ride can be done in all four seasons. You might carry insect repellent in the early summer and late fall. The off-season is a good time to visit Martha's Vineyard since it's less expensive and the weather is milder than on the mainland. Between Memorial Day and Labor Day, the roads on the island (as well as Cape Cod) are busier.

**Services:** All services are available in Vineyard Haven, Oak Bluffs, and other towns. Cycle Works is a shop in Vineyard Haven, about 1 mile from the ferry landing. There is no camping in the state park, but there are two private campgrounds on the island.

**Hazards:** Watch out for the occasional hiker or horseback rider. Also, in early spring and late fall, ticks can be hiding in the woods, so it's recommended not to wander into the underbrush. There's some poison ivy among the blueberry bushes.

**Rescue index:** At most you will be about 2 miles from assistance on easily traversed but secluded roads and trails.

**Land status:** Trails and fire lanes in a state park.

**Maps:** A good map of the roads and many of the trails on the Vineyard is called "Martha's Vineyard," published by Vineyard native J. Donovan; available in many stores on the island. Some of the trails in the state park appear only in this book.

**Finding the trail:** If you're visiting the island, you get there by boat. There is a ferry from Woods Hole on the southwestern tip of Cape Cod, which arrives in the town of Vineyard Haven. The ferry leaves almost every 45 minutes, from 7:15 A.M. to 10:15 P.M., year-round. (See the Appendix under "Steamship Authority.") The ferry parking lot at Woods Hole can easily fill up. Instead, you can pay to park in a lot 4 miles away with shuttle service. Or, as some cyclists do, park in a legal spot anywhere on Cape Cod and bike to the ferry.

Once you're at the ferry landing in Vineyard Haven, you can take either the

Riding on a divided "highway." Martha's Vineyard, Massachusetts.

main roads to the state park (South Main Street and Edgartown Road) or, if you have a map, explore some of the less-traveled roads along Lagoon Pond, then hook up with Edgartown Road. It's about 3.5 miles from the ferry landing to the state park.

On Edgartown Road, heading south, you will reach a major four-way intersection with a blinking light. Turn right onto Airport Road, and the state park sign and access road will soon come up on the left.

**Sources of additional information:** Manuel F. Correllus (Martha's Vineyard) State Forest and Vineyard Offroad Bicycling Association (see Appendix).

**Notes on the trail:** Although there are quite a few turns on this ride, as long as you stay oriented north-south and east-west—using the grid of fire lanes—you shouldn't become lost for too long. Begin by riding up the paved access road and forking left (to the right is the ranger's driveway). Go through a forest gate on the right, past a fire lane on the left. Take the next fire lane bearing left.

You will reach a large field; pick up a narrow, grassy trail on the left side of the field, just behind a tree line. This trail, Dr. Fisher Road, will become much more obvious. Cross another fire lane, then turn right onto the second one. Turn right on the next fire lane. You will come out at a large field. Just after the field, turn left onto a single-track trail.

Just before you reach the bike path next to a paved road, turn right onto another single-track trail. This trail comes out at a paved road. Make a dogleg turn to the left and right on the pavement, and pick up the bike path along the paved road. Ride past the airport, and just after the airport, turn right at a fence onto a trail. You will come out on the bike path again; turn right. When the path veers to the left, bear right onto a fire lane. Just after descending over a hill, turn sharply left onto a single-track trail, and bear to the right.

The trail will end at a wide fire lane. Turn right, and you will reach a small clearing with the bike path crossing it. Pick up the bike path heading in the same direction, cross another fire lane, and turn right (south) on the next fire lane. You will reach a junction at the northwest corner of the airport. Turn left, pick up the bike path going in the same direction, and then turn left onto a single-track trail just before you reach Airport Road.

This trail comes out at a field. Turn left onto a double-track trail that degrades into a single-track on the other side of the field. At the tree line, take a right fork into the woods. Bear right at the next Y junction, and reach a T junction with the next fire road. Turn right, and you will come out on Airport Road. Cross the road and pick up a trail that soon comes out at the forest headquarters.

# RIDE 37 *MARTHA'S VINEYARD STATE PARK / TOUR II*

This twisting, turning 19-mile ride is a grand tour of a tranquil park in the middle of Martha's Vineyard. It's also the loop of an annual off-road ride held in the spring, which draws several hundred cyclists. The ride is made up of about 6.5 miles of wide fire lanes, 10.5 miles of single-track and narrow double-track trails, and 2 miles of paved bike path. Expect to get lost a few times on it—but there's always an intersecting fire road to reorient yourself.

This land mass is officially named the Manuel F. Correllus State Forest, after its superintendent for 50 years. But locals call it simply by the name of this well-known island, just off the Massachusetts coastline.

Despite its sandy environment, most of the park's trails and fire lanes are easily rideable. All of the park's trails are open for biking. Still, a local ride organizer offers these tips for biking on sandier terrain: "Keep your weight back and steer lightly." He also reminds cyclists not to surprise hikers, and if you encounter horseback riders, stop and let them pass; talking around horses can also make them feel at ease.

If you're visiting the park on a Sunday, you might encounter a group ride, since the Vineyard Offroad Bicycling Association (VORBA; see Appendix) has been holding Sunday rides here for more than 10 years. Hooking up with them is a good way to become familiar with these many trails.

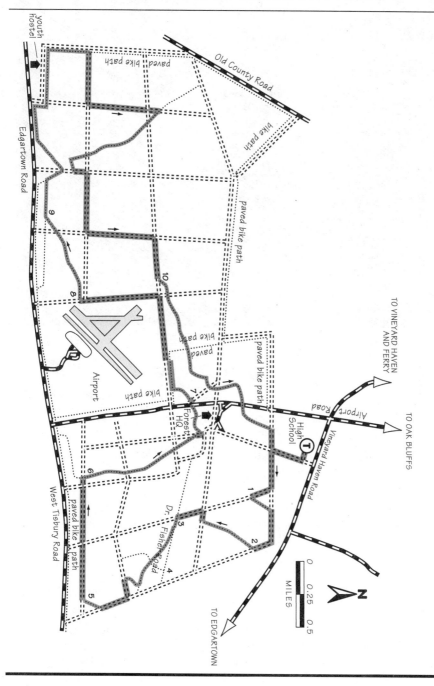

Crossing a secluded field. Martha's Vineyard State Park, Martha's Vineyard, Massachusetts.

**General location:** In the middle of Martha's Vineyard, 3.5 miles south of the ferry landing in the town of Vineyard Haven.

**Elevation change:** The terrain is flat, with occasional short dips and hills.

**Seasons:** This ride can be done in all four seasons. You might carry insect repellent in the early summer and late fall. The off-season is a good time to visit Martha's Vineyard since it's less expensive and the weather is milder than on the mainland. Also, between Memorial Day and Labor Day, the roads on the island (as well as Cape Cod) are busier.

**Services:** All services are available in Vineyard Haven, Oak Bluffs, and other towns. Cycle Works is a shop in Vineyard Haven, about 1 mile from the ferry landing. There is no camping in the state park, but there are two private campgrounds on the island.

**Hazards:** Watch out for the occasional hiker or horseback rider. Also, in early spring and late fall, ticks can be living in the woods, so it's recommended not to wander into the underbrush. There's some poison ivy among the blueberry bushes.

**Rescue index:** At most you will be about 2 miles from assistance on easily traversed but secluded roads and trails.

**Land status:** Trails and fire lanes in a state park.

**Maps:** A good map of the roads and many of the trails on the Vineyard is called "Martha's Vineyard," published by Vineyard native J. Donovan; available in many stores on the island. Some of the trails in the state park appear only in this book.

**Finding the trail:** If you're visiting the island, you get there by boat. There is a ferry from Woods Hole on the southwestern tip of Cape Cod leaving almost every 45 minutes, from 7:15 A.M. to 10:15 P.M., year-round ($10 round trip, $3 per bike one way), which arrives in the town of Vineyard Haven. (See the Appendix under "Steamship Authority" for more information.) The ferry parking lot at Woods Hole can easily fill up. Instead, you can park in a lot 4 miles away ($6 per day) with shuttle service. Or, as some cyclists do, park in a legal spot anywhere on Cape Cod and bike to the ferry.

Once you're at the ferry landing in Vineyard Haven, you can take either the main roads to the state park (South Main Street and Edgartown Road) or, if you have a map, explore some of the less-traveled roads along Lagoon Pond, then hook up with Edgartown Road. It's about 3.5 miles from the ferry landing to the state park.

On Edgartown Road, heading south, you will reach a major four-way intersection with a blinking light. Turn right onto Airport Road, and the state park sign and access road will soon come up on the left.

**Sources of additional information:** Manuel F. Correllus (Martha's Vineyard) State Forest and Vineyard Offroad Bicycling Association (see Appendix).

**Notes on the trail:** This ride has *many* turns on it. This is not to confuse cyclists, but rather to introduce them to different trails in the forest—especially lesser-known single-track ones. Don't feel compelled to do every trail. A regular grid of fire lanes throughout the forest, a paved bike path on one side, and other bordering roads will also help you stay oriented.

The tour begins at the Martha's Vineyard Regional High School, just north of the park. From the front of the school, turn right (south) out of the parking lot on to the road. After 0.3 mile, turn left on the first fire lane. After about another 0.3 mile, turn right on another fire lane.

After another 0.3 mile or so, look for a small pile of rocks and an entrance to a single-track trail on the left (1) (see map). This is about 0.9 mile into the ride (from the high school). Follow this single-track trail to the end, and turn right onto another fire lane. Follow the lane until it begins to bear right and downhill under powerlines.

Now look for another single-track trail going into the woods on the right (2). Follow this trail as it twists through the woods, staying on the main, well-worn trail. Then turn right onto a fire lane, and left at the next fire lane intersection. Follow the lane for around a quarter mile, and turn left onto a single-track trail (3); this is around 2.6 miles into the ride.

(*Note:* The following turn onto a single-track trail is trickier—it can be skipped and instead you can stay on the fire roads.) Follow this trail about three-quarters of a mile, taking a right into a pine stand (4). If you come out on a fire lane on a powerline, you've gone about 0.1 mile past it. Now you weave around the woods, bearing left onto a logging road, overgrown into a single-track trail, and after about a half mile, come out on a fire lane. Turn left and follow it to the eastern edge of the forest. Turn right on the powerline or the single-track trail next to it. Follow the powerline for around a half mile and look for an opening into the woods on your right. (If you make it to a parking area in the southeast corner of the park, you've gone slightly too far.) Follow this single-track trail until you come into a clearing and see a paved bike path on your left (5); this is about 4.9 miles into the ride. Follow the trail across the clearing into the trees, until you come out to a fire lane. Cross the lane and continue on the trail. (You can also take the bike path.)

Follow this trail across another fire lane, until you come to a single-track trail/bridle path heading northward (6). Turn right on it and follow the trail north—crossing a sandy fire lane, passing an old windmill tower, coming out of the woods and into a clearing, and going straight until the trail turns into a dirt road/fire lane. You will see buildings and equipment at the headquarters.

The next section is a fairly complicated 0.75 mile heading westward to Airport Road—you can opt for an easier route. After passing the head-quarters buildings, turn sharply left onto a narrow jeep road. Take the next right onto a narrow wooded road (a large electric utility box is on the left). Following this narrow road through the woods, you will come to an intersection in a clearing. Go straight. Take the next right turn onto an even narrower road. Follow this road for a short distance, and watch for a single-track trail bearing to the left into a valley. Follow this single-track as it winds down a hill, until it crosses a narrow, sandy jeep road. Take a left onto this road for a short distance to paved Airport Road (7); this is about 7.8 miles into the ride.

Cross Airport Road (also called Barnes Road) and the bike path, and cross a field, staying to the left by the treeline. Go between the posts in the ground on a single-track trail. Follow this trail to the left, and you will come out on the bike path. Cross the path and take a right on the dirt road. Follow this road westward, until you reach a four-way intersection (at the northwest boundary of the airport). Turn left and follow the dirt road south, go through the next intersection, and take the first right onto a single-track trail (8)—this is about 9.5 miles into the ride.

Follow this trail for about 1 mile to a fire lane. Cross the lane and continue on the trail until it intersects another single-track trail. Turn right (9). Follow this trail until you come out on the paved bike path. Turn right on the path—this is about 10.8 miles into the ride.

Now the ride becomes easier to follow, since it uses mainly the bike path and fire lanes for the next 7 miles or so. When you reach the fire lane heading north from the northwest edge of the airport, look for a single-track trail on the right (10), which eventually comes out onto a fire lane and bike path.

This next stretch is not well-mapped. You can turn right on the fire lane for a short distance and pick up a single-track trail on the left. It weaves and forks, heading northeast toward the headquarters, then around it on the northern side, and back to the northern border of the forest and the high school. (You can also take fire lanes and roads back to the high school.)

# CONNECTICUT

# Western Connecticut

## RIDE 38 HUNTINGTON STATE PARK

This undeveloped park has little in it—except for secluded woods, a lake, three ponds, a lagoon, and around 10 miles of trails. You can do short, easy rides that encircle bodies of water or more challenging loops on longer, more rugged trails (see "Caution" under Notes on the trail). Coming or going from the trailhead, though, be sure to take the path along the western border of the park, which runs through a highland field with a view.

Along the trails, watch for large, handsome bushes with dark green leaves. This is mountain laurel—its blossoms are the state flower of Connecticut. And keep an eye out for equestrians since a horse farm borders the park to the north. If you pass a horse, it's always best to stop, since some horses can be frightened by creatures with human torsos and two-wheeled bodies.

Nearby Putnam Memorial Park also has some trails.

**General location:** The town of Redding, about 8 miles southeast of Danbury.

**Elevation change:** The terrain here is relatively flat, but with many short, steep climbs and descents, some made more challenging by loose terrain.

**Seasons:** It can be a four-season ride, but avoid riding in wet weather.

**Services:** There are no amenities in the park itself. All services are available in Bethel and Danbury, including two mountain-bike shops: Bethel Cycle in Bethel and Bike Express in Danbury.

**Hazards:** Since the trails are unmarked, one can get disoriented, especially going further from the trailhead. (A compass will help.) Watch out for loose gravel and heavily eroded areas on some descents. Yield to horseback riders and avoid scaring hikers. Announce yourself in plenty of time.

**Rescue index:** At most you will be about 1 mile from assistance.

**Land status:** State park trails.

**Maps:** *Note:* This undeveloped park is not well-mapped, and there has been new housing and road construction on some of its borders. You might be able to pick up a map at a local bike shop or from the state Department of Environmental Protection (see Appendix).

**Finding the trail:** From Connecticut Highway 15 (the Merritt Parkway), take Exit 44 onto CT 58, heading north toward Redding. After about 10.5 miles,

# RIDE 38  *HUNTINGTON STATE PARK*

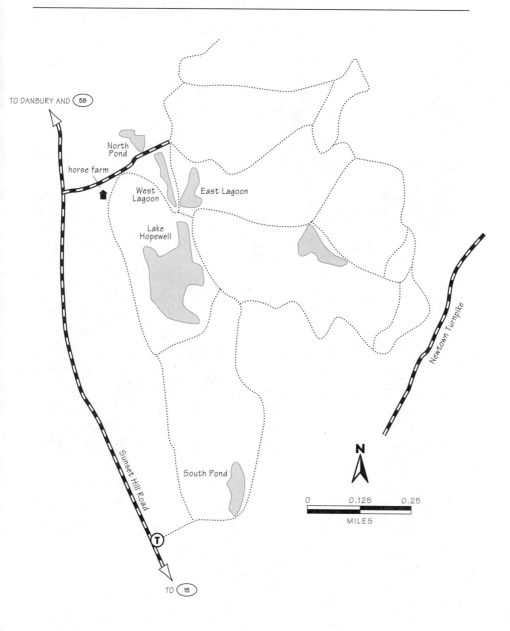

TO DANBURY AND 58

North Pond

horse farm

West Lagoon

East Lagoon

Lake Hopewell

Newtown Turnpike

Sunset Hill Road

South Pond

N

0    0.125    0.25

MILES

T

TO 15

Announcing the trailhead. Huntington State Park, Redding, Connecticut.

turn right onto Sunset Hill Road and watch for an unmarked parking area on the right (with two stone pillars).

From the north, take Exit 5 on Interstate 84, onto CT 53 east, toward Danbury. Head south through Danbury on CT 53 (Main Street). After 2.5 miles, turn left onto CT 302, then right onto CT 58 south, and left onto Sunset Hill Road. After a couple of miles, you will reach the parking area on the left.

**Sources of additional information:** The state Bureau of Outdoor Recreation, Department of Environmental Protection (see Appendix).

**Notes on the trail:** You can take many different rides in this park by connecting different loops. *Caution:* The trails are unmarked, and the area is not well-mapped, although it is relatively compact. If you decide to explore trails farther away from the ponds and the lake, bring a compass and expect to reach private property and roads in new developments.

The trail heading straight down from the parking area is steep and eroded. For a scenic, gentle beginning, turn left at the trailhead and cruise through an open field; then veer right and descend into the woods. To familiarize yourself with the park, you might first circumvent the three ponds, then explore longer, more secluded loops to the east.

# RIDE 39 *TRUMBULL / OLD MINE PARK*

This moderate 11-mile loop connects four distinctly different trails: a 3.5-mile rail-trail, a 1.5-mile loop around an old mine (now a park), a 2-mile cart path, and a more challenging 2.5-mile single-track trail along a river. In addition to the ride in this book, there are several technical single-track trails snaking off the cart path to the east. Each section of the ride can also be done separately.

The flat, wooded double-track rail-trail of packed dirt and gravel runs next to a gorge with a lively river tumbling down it. At the northern end of this former railbed, you reach Old Mine Park, a popular recreation area, with some fields and a rugged loose-gravel trail climbing past an old mine site.

Then, after riding on pavement for about a mile, you arrive at the other side of the river, where there is another park, Indian Ledge Park. This one has a BMX racetrack in it (which is usually closed except for race day). The next section heads into deep pine woods on an old cart path that follows a ridge above the single-track trail. And for adventurous side trips, keep an eye out for single-track trails that intersect this trail to the east.

After following the cart path for about 2 miles, you will come to the remains of an old reservoir (drained in 1935). Skirting the perimeter of the field to the right, you meet up with the single-track trail, and veer northward again. This

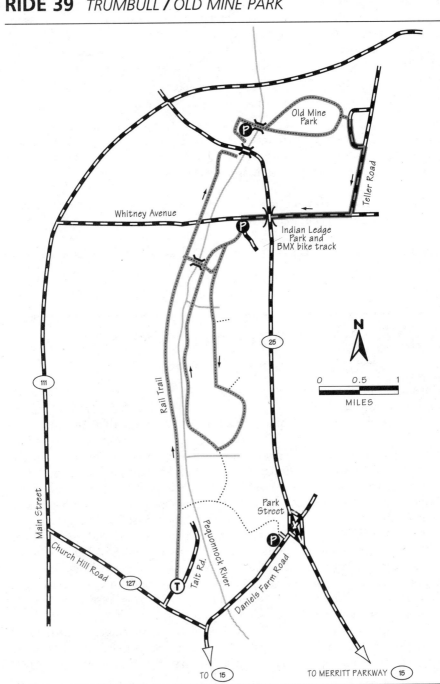

Old Mine Park

Teller Road

Whitney Avenue

Indian Ledge Park and BMX bike track

111

25

Rail Trail

N

0    0.5    1
MILES

Main Street

Church Hill Road

127

T

Tait Rd.

Pequonnock River

Park Street

Daniels Farm Road

TO  15

TO MERRITT PARKWAY  15

rugged trail, which follows the river, passes over rocks and roots and finally reaches a bridge to reconnect with the rail-trail.

**General location:** Just north of the town of Trumbull, off Connecticut Highway 25.

**Elevation change:** The terrain is flat, except for a short, steep climb on a loose-gravel jeep road (in Old Mine Park) and a steep descent on pavement leaving the park.

**Seasons:** Any time between late spring and late fall is good.

**Services:** All services are available on CT 127 and in Trumbull.

**Hazards:** Be ready to change riding techniques when switching from flat, smooth trails to pavement, then to technical single-track. Also, watch out for traffic on a highway that you must cross after a steep descent (just before Indian Ledge Park). As always, watch for hikers and other cyclists on the trails. Some hunting is allowed in areas around the river in hunting season (late November and December).

**Rescue index:** At most you will be about a quarter mile from assistance

**Land status:** Public trails and a former railroad bed. (The river valley was purchased for public use in 1989 for $9.2 million.)

**Maps:** The parks and cross-streets will appear on a detailed road map. Detailed maps of the trails may be available at the trailheads on Tait Road and Whitney Avenue. These maps provide a colorful description of the historical significance of the rail-trail and points of interest within the combined Pequonnock Valley, Indian Ledge, Parlor Rock, and Old Mine Park.

**Finding the trail:** From CT 15 (the Merritt Parkway), take the Trumbull/Route 127 exit and head north toward Trumbull on White Plains Road. After 1.3 miles, just after crossing CT 25, turn right onto Tait Road. After a few hundred feet, you will see the trail forking uphill on the left, behind some boulders. Park off the road.

From CT 25, take Exit 9 onto Daniels Farm Road. At the light in Trumbull, turn right onto Tait Road. You can also begin riding on the single-track trail and cart path from the commuter parking lot along CT 25 or off Whitney Avenue. To reach the commuter lot, after getting off CT 25, take the first right off Daniels Farm Road onto Park Street. The commuter lot is just past the entrance to CT 25, and the trail begins at the end of Park Street.

**Sources of additional information:** The *Hometown Publications* newspaper has published a historical guidebook for this area. Copies may be obtained by writing to the newspaper (see Appendix).

**Notes on the trail:** After about 1 mile on the rail-trail (which was part of the Housatonic Railroad until 1932), you will pass a double-track trail forking down to the right, toward the river. For a technical ride, take this fork across the river and head north on the single-track trail and cart path. Otherwise, after about 2.5 miles on the rail-trail, you cross paved Whitney Avenue. Shortly afterward, you will pass Parlor Rock Park, the site of an amusement park in the nineteenth century; today only trees and a plaque remain.

Now comes a tricky junction: Just before reaching CT 25, fork off the rail-trail onto a single-track trail on the right. Stay in the woods, riding along the highway, and soon veer left underneath the highway bridge, then left again, and onto a trail that parallels the highway. The trail widens into the rail-trail again and comes out at a paved parking area at Old Mine Park. Cross the footbridge in the park, and ride into the woods on a loose-gravel jeep road.

This jeep road goes up a three-quarter mile climb over loose gravel and rocks, and may be followed all the way around for a fast downhill. Be careful on the downhill, though; there are two drop-offs not recommended for the faint of heart. Then continue doing the loop on the map, following the jeep trail up the hill, and then fork off it on the east side onto a trail that soon reaches a paved road.

Turn right on the pavement, right onto paved Skating Pond Road, and right again onto paved Teller Road. After a steep downhill, you will reach a T junction at Whitney Avenue.

Turn right, ride under CT 25, and turn left almost immediately onto a paved road with a sign at it for Indian Ledge Park. (You can ride on this access road to a BMX racetrack, which is up a hill.) Look for the start of the cart path, which begins below the playground. Follow this double-track trail through the woods, across a small stream, and over a small drop-off. The trail bears left to a short, technical downhill with many rocks and roots. At the end of this downhill, turn left immediately up a hill to a ridge overlooking a former reservoir basin. Follow the trail down the hill and to the right around the perimeter of the field.

As you approach the river, turn right and head back up north on the single-track trail. This section of trail hugs the river's edge and can be technical and muddy if it has rained recently. A little over a mile from the reservoir basin, you will reach a bridge that crosses the river to the left and leads back up to the rail-trail. Turn left on the rail-trail and follow it back to the trailhead at Tait Road.

# RIDE 40 *NEPAUG STATE FOREST*

This is a small forest of 1,100 acres that's packed with single-track trails and narrow dirt roads weaving through sandy terrain and an abundance of pine trees. Local riders maintain a moderately challenging 5-mile loop on the single-track trails and dirt roads, or you can do an easier ride by staying on the roads.

Another favorite ride in this forest takes the Tunxis Trail northward to Satan's Kingdom and a lookout to the west. You can also extend this ride

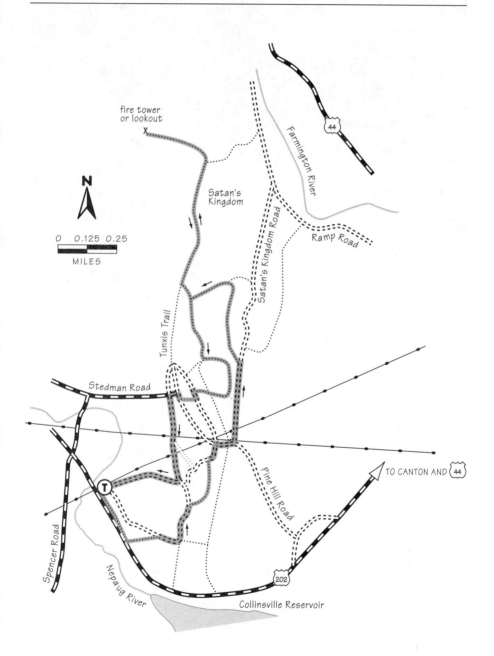

Fast cruising on hard-packed sand. Nepaug State Forest, New Hartford, Connecticut.

by forking off the Tunxis Trail at the northern end of the loop onto other twisting trails, including a fun descent to the Farmington River. There's good swimming on the river, near Satan's Kingdom Road. The river is also a favorite spot for tubing.

**General location:** Near the town of New Hartford, 4.5 miles west of Canton and 20 miles west of Hartford.

**Elevation change:** This ride rolls up and down between 550 feet and 700 feet, and alternates between short, steep climbs and longer, more gradual ones.

**Seasons:** Any time between late spring and winter.

**Services:** All services are available in Canton and along U.S. Highway 44. There's a bike shop, Benidorm (formerly Summit Mountain Bike), on US 44 in Canton.

**Hazards:** Watch out for some obstructions on the tighter single-track trails and some soft spots on the sand-surfaced roads. Expect some bugs in wet weather. And wear bright clothing during hunting season in late fall.

**Rescue index:** At most you will be about 1.5 miles from a traveled road.

**Land status:** An active town road and roads and trails in a state forest.

**Maps:** A map may be available at Benidorm bike shop on US 44 in Canton, or contact the state Bureau of Outdoor Recreation (see Appendix).

**Finding the trail:** From the junction of US 202 and US 44, just west of Canton, head west on US 202. At 2.8 miles, turn right onto a narrow, unpaved road with a sign: "Nepaug State Forest." A few hundred feet up the road, park at turnoffs under the pine trees.

**Sources of additional information:** Bureau of Outdoor Recreation, Department of Environmental Protection (see Appendix).

**Notes on the trail:** There are many turns on this compact 5-mile ride, which uses a red-blazed loop maintained by local mountain bikers. You can familiarize yourself with the layout of the forest by first exploring the dirt roads that interconnect within it.

To do the 5-mile loop, begin by forking immediately onto a single-track trail on the right side of the dirt road at the trailhead. You will reach the dirt road after less than a half mile. Turn right on it and, on a downhill, fork right into the woods. You will come out at a jeep road; turn left on it (heading north). At a three-way intersection with an island, dogleg right and left, and cross a power line. You're now on Satan's Kingdom Road.

*A tricky turn:* Watch for a single-track trail heading into the woods on the left, up an embankment. Take it, fork right almost immediately, then dogleg left and right on the trail. You will reach a logging clearing; turn left uphill. You join another wider trail, the Tunxis Trail. You can turn right on it to reach a lookout. Or veer left and, after a downhill, reach a gate and continue straight ahead. At a four-way intersection, turn left. After a downhill, you reach a three-way intersection at a clearing and turn right. Cross a dirt road and reach another road, where you turn right. Follow this road back to the trailhead.

# RIDE 41 *WEST HARTFORD RESERVOIR*

This fairly challenging 8-mile loop explores a favorite site for mountain biking near Hartford, the state capital. The heart of the ride runs for several miles along a ridge, then returns on other single-track trails in the woods, or you can take an easier route using secluded dirt roads.

Single- and double-track trails make up most of this ride, with a few stretches on woods roads. From the well-maintained reservoir area, it's a short climb to a wooded ridge, with a side trip to a lookout.

The paved roads skirting the reservoirs are also popular walking areas. The Metropolitan District Commission (MDC), which manages the reservoir area, asks that cyclists avoid riding on them, if possible. If you must use these roads

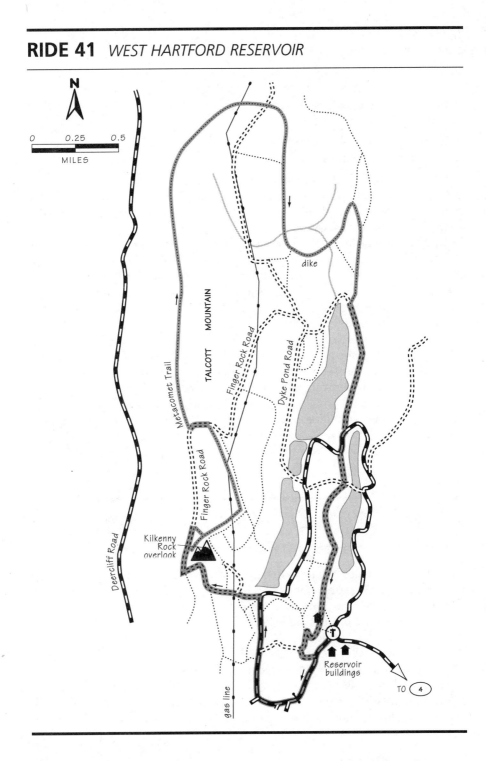

N

0        0.25        0.5

MILES

dike

TALCOTT  MOUNTAIN

Finger Rock Road

Dyke Pond Road

Metacomet Trail

Finger Rock Road

Deercliff Road

Kilkenny
Rock
overlook

gas line

Reservoir
buildings

TO 4

Coming out of the woods. West Hartford, Connecticut.

for access to the trails, follow the one-way restriction for bicycles and ride only in the painted bike lane.

**General location:** About 8 miles west of Hartford.

**Elevation change:** The ride begins with a fairly steep climb of about 400 feet. Afterward, you will cruise along a ridge, then descend gradually.

**Seasons:** This can be a four-season ride, but expect plenty of mud in the spring and after a rainfall.

**Services:** All services are available along Connecticut Highway 4 and in West Hartford. A bike shop is Central Wheel Bike Shop on CT 4 near the reservoir entrance (see Ride 42 for other local bike shops).

**Hazards:** Watch for occasional obstructions on the single-track trails. Also, avoid startling walkers—announce yourself when approaching from behind.

**Rescue index:** At most you will be about 1 mile from assistance on secluded trails. (The area is patrolled by members of the New England Mountain Bike Patrol, who are trained in First Aid and CPR and inform MDC and emergency personnel of problems via cell phones.)

**Land status:** MDC trails and woods roads. Most of the trails here are open for multiple use; adhere to the few closures.

**Maps:** You can buy a detailed trail map near the trailhead (in the Filter Plant Administration Building, which is the closest building to CT 4). A copy of this map is posted on a board in the main parking lot.

**Finding the trail:** From CT 4 in West Hartford, turn right into the reservoir area at two large stone pillars and a large sign, "West Hartford Water Treatment Plant." Fork right on the access road, pass several buildings, and reach a large parking area.

**Sources of additional information:** The Central Wheel bike shop near the entrance on CT 4 (Farmington Avenue) posts trail conditions and other useful information.

**Notes on the trail:** There are some long, secluded trails and woods roads in this area. It might be useful to bring along the detailed map available at the administration building (see Maps). You might also want to carry a compass.

To reach the ridge, head south from the parking area on a paved road. Follow the road through a gate and stay to the right in the bike lane. Continue circling to the right on the paved road, until it climbs a small hill and you see a reservoir on your left. Turn left onto a patchy asphalt road at a junction marked with a map board, and climb.

After a half mile or so, turn right onto a rugged road. (For an easier ride, just continue on this road, Finger Rock Road.) Veer right onto a trail and climb to a lookout (Kilkenny Rock).

Descend back to the jeep road and turn right, soon reaching a gas pipeline trail. Turn left on that trail and almost immediately right, crossing the gas pipeline and forking left onto a trail that parallels the gas line (the right fork leads to another view). You cross the gas line again, then turn left onto a dirt road at a T junction. Turn sharply right at a fork onto another dirt road. At a wide clearing at a power line, fork left onto a single-track trail. This is the blue-blazed Metacomet Trail, a major north-south trail.

You cross the gas line again about 5 miles into the ride, now heading west to east. Then you will soon cross a road; staying on the cleared trail, fork right (south) at the next turn. (You can reach more trails toward Talcott Mountain to the north by turning left on the road.) Veer to the left, and you will reach a fork at a large clearing.

At this point, two trails head south. One option is to veer left across the clearing and a flood control dike. After a couple of mud holes, turn right onto a single-track trail. (If you miss this turn, you will reach a field and U.S. Highway 44.) At a four-way intersection with a fence on the other side, turn right.

Almost immediately, veer left and follow a single-track trail that will follow the fence on your left. Go across a small, tarred road, and continue until this trail ends at a paved road around the reservoirs. Go left, staying in the marked bike lane and you will soon reach the parking area.

# RIDE 42 *PENNWOOD STATE PARK*

This moderate 8.5-mile ride is a sampling of the "highs" and "lows" in this beautiful, forested state park. All trails in this long, narrow park are open for cycling, except for this section of the blue-blazed Metacomet Trail, which runs down the center of the park. Although not difficult riding, the scenic trail to the west runs along the edge of some cliffs, where cyclists should use common sense. There's also a stunning vista along the western ridge.

To do an easier, shorter ride, you can take just the southern loop, using an old, patchy asphalt trail from the parking area to Lake Louise and back. Another option is to do the western half of the ride as an out-and-back excursion—recommended after wet weather. On the southeastern side of the ride, you can stop and relax at some picnic sites.

**General location:** Around 9 miles northwest of Hartford, off Connecticut Highway 185.

**Elevation change:** You begin at 425 feet, climb gradually and steadily to 550 feet, then descend.

**Seasons:** Summer and fall are the best seasons. The northeastern trail can be muddy; retracing one's route along the western ridge is recommended during wet weather.

**Services:** All services are available along U.S. Highway 44, including Benidorm bike shop (formerly Summit Mountain Bike) in Canton on US 44, the Bicycle Cellar on Hop Meadow Street in Simsbury, and Bloomfield Bicycle on Seneca Road in Bloomfield.

**Hazards:** The trail to the west sometimes approaches the edges of cliffs—use caution. Less-experienced riders should not attempt to ride over all obstacles on the single-track trails. The asphalt "trail" to Lake Louise has some sunken sewer grates in it; ride on the sides.

**Rescue index:** You will be about 2 miles from assistance on well-used trails.

**Land status:** Trails in a state park. Metacomet Trail, the blue-blazed trail through the center of the park, is closed to cyclists.

**Maps:** USGS, 7.5 minute series, Avon, CT.

**Finding the trail:** On CT 185, about 8 miles west of Hartford and about 2 miles east of CT 10, watch for signs on the north for Pennwood State Park. Turn into the paved parking lot, which is just off CT 185.

**Sources of additional information:** Bureau of Outdoor Recreation, Department of Environmental Protection (see Appendix), or ask at a local bike shop (see Services above).

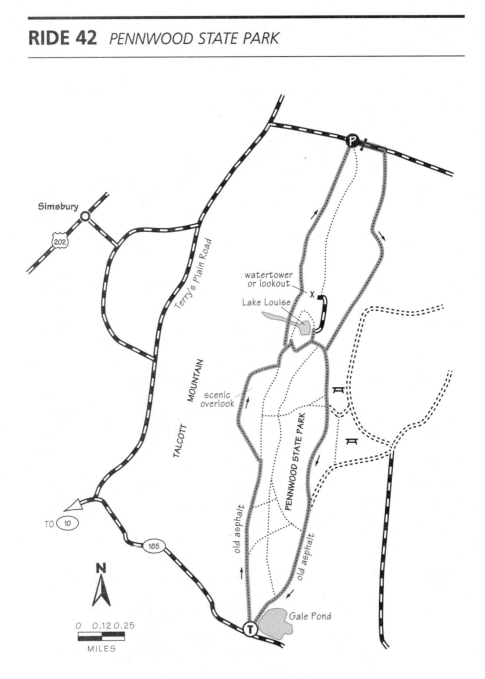

Simsbury

202

Terry's Plain Road

watertower
or lookout

Lake Louise

scenic
overlook

TALCOTT MOUNTAIN

PENNWOOD STATE PARK

old asphalt

old asphalt

TO 10

185

N

0   0.12  0.25
MILES

Gale Pond

Board riding. Pennwood State Park, Simsbury, Connecticut.

**Notes on the trail:** Pick up a narrow asphalt "trail" on the north side of the parking lot, taking the left fork. Follow this old path as it climbs gently for about 0.6 mile. Turn sharply left onto a single-track trail, cross a small wooded bridge (built by the local mountain-bike chapter), and climb slowly to the ridge. When the trail descends and rejoins the asphalt path, turn left on the path.

Soon, turn left onto a narrow dirt road, following it until it reaches a T junction with a jeep trail. Turn left on the trail, climbing toward the ridge again. The trail becomes wider and gradually descends toward the northern edge of the park. It comes out at an asphalt cul-de-sac with a parking area. In wet weather or after heavy rains, it is best to retrace your ride on this trail, rather than completing the muddier loop to the east.

Otherwise, turn right on the road, pass through a gate, and almost immediately turn right uphill on a double-track trail. This trail will eventually bring you back to the asphalt loop trail just east and a bit south of Lake Louise. You can take this path southward back to the parking area or turn right onto trails connecting in the middle of the park (but do not ride on the blue-blazed Metacomet Trail). *Caution:* The center of this paved "trail" has old storm sewer grates sunken deeply in it—ride on either the left or right side of the path.

# RIDE 43 *WEST ROCK RIDGE STATE PARK*

This prominent, extended ridge on the outskirts of New Haven has been a long-time haven for local residents. The area's first inhabitants, Native Americans, not only hunted along its steep slopes, but also wintered on the eastern side to protect themselves from bitter northwest winds. Later, in the 1660s, two British justices, William Goffe and Edward Whalley, hid out on the ridge after they had alienated their king, Charles I—by signing his death warrant.

In the 1880s, the city of New Haven began developing West Rock into a park, building not only trails but a carriage road to the top of the ridge. Even then, the road was recognized as a marvel of engineering, with its gentle grades created by switchbacks.

Today, the park's 1,500 acres are a quiet spot in the city for cyclists, hikers, and bird watchers, who all take advantage of the secluded trails and scenic roads just a few miles from major highways.

"We've got both extremes here," says West Rock park supervisor and mountain biker Alex Sokolow, "smoother, flatter trails and roads—and extreme, technical trails."

Since many of the longer trails and the park road run along the ridge rather than across it, there's less climbing here than one might expect. And even mountain bikers should be sure to explore the paved park road—which is closed to cars, except for a stretch to the lookout area at the southern tip on weekends. At the lookout area, one can enjoy an unobstructed view of New Haven and the surrounding land. Cruising on Baldwin Drive (named after one of its benefactors and a former governor of Connecticut) affords more scenic views.

Other mellower rides in the park surround Lake Wintergreen and follow the flat Red Trail from Mountain Road to the parking area. On the other hand, exploring the single-track trails, especially in the southern section, will challenge most cyclists with its embedded rock and steep inclines.

The park is open from 8 A.M. to sunset.

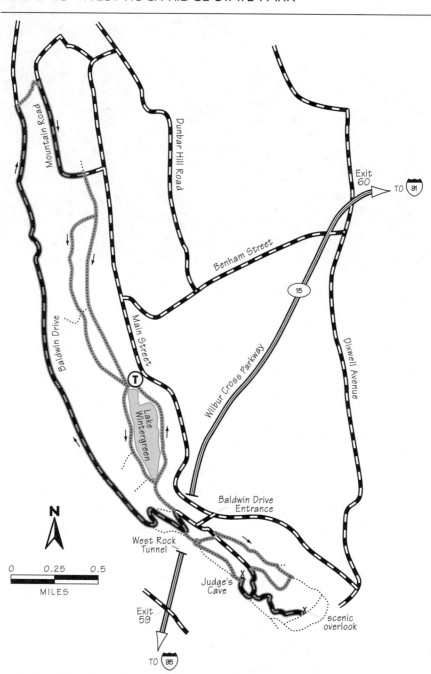

Comparing notes at an overlook between hikers and the park supervisor (a mountain biker). West Rock Ridge State Park, New Haven, Connecticut.

**General location:** Towns of New Haven and Hamden, 2 miles from the Wilber Cross Parkway (Connecticut Highway 15).

**Elevation change:** Depending on which trails and/or roads you take, there's a moderate amount of climbing—or a bit more. In general, the longer trails and road running north-south are flat. The single-track trails in the southern part of the park have some short, steep (and technical) climbs. It's a steady, fairly easy climb on the paved road to the lookout and/or ridge.

**Seasons:** Summer and fall are best. Spring can be wet.

**Services:** All services are available along CT 15 and in Hamden and New Haven. A local bike shop is Amity Bicycle off Exit 5 on CT 15.

**Hazards:** Some stretches of the single-track trails should be attempted only by experienced riders; others can walk them. Always watch out for hikers on the trails, as well as occasional obstructions. On weekends, motorized vehicles are allowed on the stretch of paved Baldwin Drive that climbs to the lookout and Judge's Cave.

**Rescue index:** At most you will be about 1.5 miles from a traveled road or trailhead.

**Land status:** Trails and roads on public land. Note: Several of the trails, including the Blue Trail paralleling Baldwin Drive, are reserved for hiking.

**Maps:** You can pick up a map at Sleeping Giant State Park, located a few miles north of West Rock Ridge State Park (on Interstate 91, take Exit 10, then head north on CT 40 and Whitney Avenue).

**Finding the trail:** Take Exit 60 on the Wilber Cross Parkway (CT 15) and head south on Dixwell Avenue. After a short distance, turn right onto Benham Street. After 2 miles, turn left onto Main Street. Then after 0.8 mile, turn right into a small parking area at the trailhead. (This is not the main park entrance; it is located a little farther south on Main Street and right onto Wintergreen Avenue.)

**Sources of additional information:** West Rock Ridge State Park, c/o Sleeping Giant State Park (see Appendix).

**Notes on the trail:** From the parking area, ride down the wide gravel path to the northern side of Lake Wintergreen. From there, you can turn south around the lake and pick up a single-track trail (Red Trail) to reach more single-track trails and the scenic overlooks. Or, head north on the Red or White trails.

To make a grand tour of the park, you can begin by riding south around the far side of the lake, and at its southern end (after 0.8 mile), fork right onto a jeep road that almost immediately becomes a single-track trail. This trail ends at stone steps that come out at a guardrail on paved Baldwin Drive (no cars are allowed on this section of the road). Climb on the road, and at the next switchback, on the other side of the guardrail, pick up another single-track trail (Green Trail). Almost immediately fork left on the trail, cross the paved road again, and then veer right on the Red Trail. *A tricky turn:* After about one-third mile, as the trail veers left at a large gully, turn right up another single-track trail that climbs steeply. After 0.2 mile, you reach the paved road again. Turn left on the road and climb to the lookout (cars are allowed on this section on weekends only).

After taking in the view, descend on the road, and fork left toward Judge's Cave. At the picnic area at the cave (it looks like a rock), take a double-track trail heading north, and almost immediately fork right on it. After about a half mile, watch for the guardrail a few yards up on the left—this is the same guardrail you crossed in the other direction.

You can then retrace the route back to Lake Wintergreen. Otherwise, turn left, climb on the paved road to the top of the ridge, and continue on scenic Baldwin Drive (no cars allowed) for about 4 miles. Look for a break in the guardrail and a single-track trail to the right (Yellow Trail). Take this trail to Mountain Road (a town road), turn right (south) on the road, following it as it bends eastward. Then look for a gate on the right, and pick up the Red Trail on the other side of it.

Now you can return to the parking area on the wide, flat, grassy Red Trail; or, after a short distance, look on the right for a single-track trail (White Trail) to do a slightly more challenging ride back to the trailhead.

# RIDE 44 *TYLER MILL RUN*

The Tyler Mill area is a large stand of woods in the midst of farmland. Many mountain bikers come here just to tackle the winding, rolling single-track trails in the southern part of this compact area. Actually, it's more like a single "ribbon" twisting through the woodscape—which makes it easy to follow. Although this popular trail—which is the site of an annual mountain-bike race—isn't much longer than 4 miles, it can seem to go on forever.

This ride begins and ends with 1.5 miles of warm-up and cool-down on double-track trails through fields and woods. To reach the single-track trails, cross a bridge over the Muddy River, where a mill once stood—now a local hangout. To do only the single-track trails, park along the roads approaching the bridge (Tyler Mill Road and Maltby Lane).

There are more trails in the woods to the west of this ride. They're unmapped, though, so you might want to hook up with a local rider to familiarize yourself with them. On the other hand, it's a fairly compact area, so if you don't mind doing a bit of road-riding, you might try exploring and seeing where you come out.

**General location:** The town of Wallingford, just off Interstate 91, about 12 miles north of New Haven.

**Elevation change:** There is one short, steep climb near the beginning of the ride from the northern trailhead, and some more gradual climbs and descents through the rest of the ride. The single-track "ribbon" at the southern end has many short climbs and descents on it.

**Seasons:** Summer and fall are best for riding.

**Services:** Services are available in the center of Wallingford, a few miles west of the ride. An active mountain bike shop is North Haven Bike on U.S. Highway 5 in North Haven.

**Hazards:** The single-track trails at the southern end are very narrow, with trees on either side—stay in control of your bike. Be sure to do the loop in the direction on the map to avoid collisions.

**Rescue index:** At most you will be about 1 mile from assistance.

**Land status:** Trails and roads managed by the town of Wallingford.

**Maps:** You might be able to get a "Dooley's Run" race map from the Parks Department in Wallingford. There is no "official" map of this area, and some of the trails are not mapped at all. You might also find a map at the New England Mountain Bike Association web site, www.nemba.org.

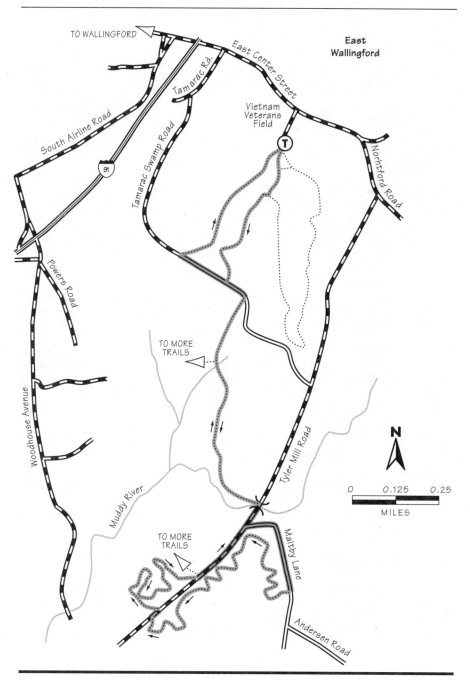

Twisting single-track riding. Wallingford, Connecticut.

**Finding the trail:** From the south, take Exit 14 on I-91 (Woodhouse Avenue/ Wallingford). Turn left and then turn right at the light onto South Airline Road. At the next light, turn right onto East Center Street, cross I-91, and soon look for the large Vietnam Veterans Field on the right. Turn right and ride to the parking area.

From the north, take Exit 14 on I-91, and turn left onto East Center Street, cross I-91 and railroad tracks, and watch for the trailhead soon on the right.

**Sources of additional information:** The Connecticut Chapter of the New England Mountain Bike Association (see Appendix, under NEMBA).

**Notes on the trail:** From the Vietnam Veterans Field parking area, three trails fan out. The far-left one begins a challenging loop, created by local mountain bikers, which eventually reconnects with the main north-south trail. The far-right trail is where this ride will come out.

Taking the center trail, you climb through a field and into the woods. Fork right and stay on the main trail, until it reaches unpaved Tamarac Swamp Road, after about 0.4 mile. Turn left on the road and after about 100 yards, look for a trail on the right, just before the road veers left. After another 0.3 mile, you will pass a short connector trail on the right, which leads to other trails.

Continuing southward, you reach Tyler Mill Road at a campfire site—a local hangout. Turn right on the road, cross the bridge, climb for just a short distance, and turn sharply left onto unpaved Maltby Lane. Now look for a single-track trailhead on the right, after about 0.1 mile, as you're climbing. This winding trail will come out on Tyler Mill Road. Turn right and pick up another trailhead on the left.

After rolling up and down in the woods on this trail, you will end up looping back to Tyler Mill Road. (You can turn back into the woods at this point to take more trails, but they're not mapped.) Otherwise, turn left onto the road and retrace your route back to Tamarac Swamp Road.

Turn left on Tamarac Swamp Road—passing the trailhead where you came out in the other direction—climb, and *just* before the road becomes paved, look for a trailhead into a field on the right (between small boulders). Turn right and follow this trail back to the parking area.

# RIDE 45  *WESTWOODS*

This 1,200-acre woods near the Atlantic Ocean has more than 40 miles of single-track trails, about half of them rideable. A few trails are easy, some are moderate, and quite a few rank as difficult. You can do an easy out-and-back ride on flat trails or a challenging 15-mile loop on rugged single-track. Be aware, though, it will take more than one visit to become familiar with the trails, and it's easy to get lost. If you take a wrong trail, you may find yourself carrying your bike up a short, steep cliff (or doubling back).

This site is a favorite spot for hiking, horseback riding, and bird watching, too. Its tight network of trails is therefore best explored at a moderate pace. Less-experienced cyclists might take the Blue Square Trail (east-west) and the Green and Orange trails (north-south). More advanced riders will want to tackle some of the narrower, steeper cross-over trails. A few trails pass through marshland, making them wet year-round—and particularly in the spring.

Be sure to obey the rules of trail etiquette here. The local trail committee has considered banning bikes several times in the past. If you live nearby, getting involved in trail maintenance is a good idea.

This area is full of ecological niches. You can enjoy marshes, hemlock forests, stands of hardwoods, deep green mountain laurel bushes, and wildflowers such as trailing arbutus. There are also more than a dozen scenic sites: vistas, prehistoric rock carvings, a waterfall, and giant rock formations called "glacial erratics." On the southern side of paved Connecticut Highway 146, the White Trail runs along a saltwater marsh near the ocean, although it's not rideable the entire way. There's more riding to the west in the Branford rock-quarry trails.

**General location:** The town of Guilford, near the junction of Interstate 95 and U.S. Highway 1, 10 miles east of New Haven and I-91.

**Elevation change:** The terrain here is relatively flat, but with some short, steep climbs.

**Seasons:** Any time except spring or after a rainfall is good for riding.

**Services:** All services are available in Guilford and along US 1.

**Hazards:** Despite its compactness and proximity to the seashore, these woods contain some technical trails. Beginners should expect to walk in places if they explore some trails; even more experienced riders must keep an eye out for hidden or sudden obstructions. Also, there can be families with children hiking, so cyclists must slow down and stop at times.

**Rescue index:** At most you will be about 1 mile from a traveled road.

**Land status:** Trails on state land, land trust, and private land.

# RIDE 45 *WESTWOODS*

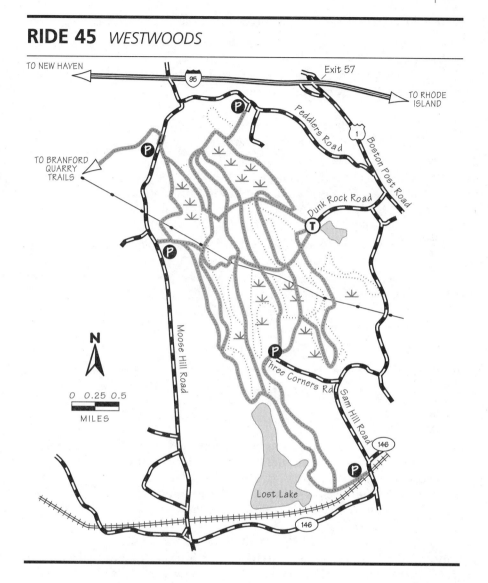

TO NEW HAVEN

95

Exit 57

TO RHODE ISLAND

Peddlers Road

1

Boston Post Road

TO BRANFORD QUARRY TRAILS

P

P

Dunk Rock Road

T

P

N

0   0.25   0.5
MILES

Moose Hill Road

Three Corners Rd

Sam Hill Road

P

146

P

146

Lost Lake

**Maps:** A detailed trail map is found in the *Connecticut Walk Book*, a well-known hiking book available in many outdoor stores or by mail from the Connecticut Forest and Parks Association (see Appendix).

**Finding the trail:** On I-95 take Exit 57, turning right onto US 1 toward Guilford. After less than a mile, across from Bishop's Orchard and Fruit Stand on the left, turn right onto Dunk Rock Road, which deadends at a parking area next to a field. Refer to the map for several other parking areas around the site, including on CT 146 and Moose Hill Road.

**Sources of additional information:** Westwoods Trails Committee (see Appendix).

**Notes on the trail:** This compact area is laced with trails, each blazed in a different color. The map here shows only the major trails. Many routes are blazed in more than one color, too, since each functions as a hiking trail and a cross-over trail. A few general guidelines:

- Do not make detours off the trails.
- Ride through muddy areas, not around them.
- Do not skid tires.
- The Blue Trail is the main east-west trail.
- The Green, Orange, White, and Violet trails run north-south.
- The Green Square and Orange Circle trails are the easiest; the White Circle Trail is more difficult; the Yellow Trail is the most difficult.
- Major routes are blazed with colored *circles*, while the *square* trails are mostly cross-over and run east-west.
- A power line intersects the area from east to west; you can use it to orient yourself.
- Take the Green Square Trail to reach the Branford's rock-quarry trail system to the west.

# RIDE 46 *WADSWORTH FALLS STATE PARK*

This attractive, well-used park near Middletown has around 6 miles of double- and single-track trails that interconnect in loops ranging from easy to challenging. *Note:* This park is also a popular walking site. The park supervisor reminds cyclists to avoid skidding or riding too fast. Damaging trails or creating conflicts with other, slower-moving users could lead to the closure of these trails to cyclists.

The easier trails in the northern half of the park wind through a handsome forest of hemlock, basswood, beech, and birch trees. A more challenging 4-mile perimeter loop takes you on the rugged Laurel Brook Trail, White Birch Trail, Cedar Loop Trail, and Main Trail to the railroad tracks. From there, a trail goes past dramatic Wadsworth Falls.

This former estate has both manmade and natural highlights, including a stone house foundation and stone bridge, some 200-year-old trees, a mammoth mountain laurel on the Main Trail (marked by a plaque), and the wide, 50-foot-high Wadsworth Falls on the Coginchaug River. There's also swimming and picnicking in the park.

For intellectual exercise, visit nearby Wesleyan University in Middletown, known for its world-class cultural offerings.

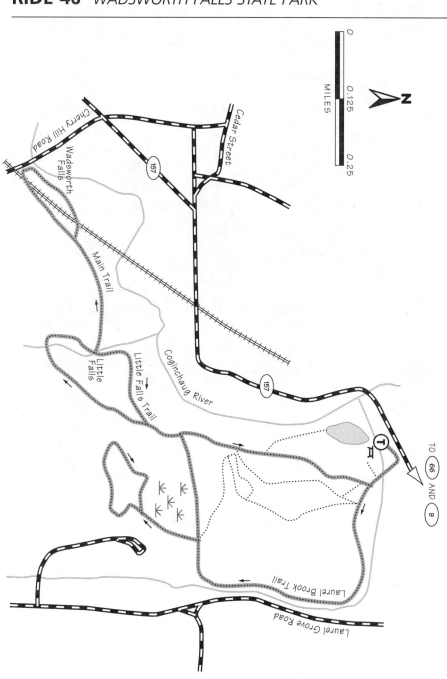

Checking out a sign at the trailhead. Wadsworth Falls State Park, Middlefield, Connecticut.

**General location:** The town of Middlefield, 3 miles southwest of Middletown.

**Elevation change:** Some of these trails have regular short, steep climbs and descents.

**Seasons:** This can be a three-season ride: summer, fall, and winter. Local riders recommend staying off the trails in March and April due to wetness.

**Services:** Water and restrooms are located at the parking lot; all other services are available in Middletown and along Connecticut Highway 66.

**Hazards:** Watch out for narrow, eroded areas along steep banks on the Laurel Brook Trail—*do not skid on them.* Always watch for other trail users.

**Rescue index:** At most you will be about a half mile from assistance.

**Land status:** State park trails.

**Maps:** Trail maps are usually stocked at the parking lot.

**Finding the trail:** On CT 9 take Exit 15, toward CT 66 and Wesleyan University. Pass through Middletown on CT 66, and turn left onto CT 157. Follow the signs for the park, which comes up on the right.

**Sources of additional information:** Wadsworth Falls State Park, c/o Chatfield Hollow State Park (see Appendix).

**Notes on the trail:** Most of the trails in this park are blazed in different colors. To do a 4-mile perimeter loop, begin by turning left at the first fork, heading away from the parking lot onto the Bridge Trail. You can then circumvent the park on the Laurel Brook Trail, White Birch Trail, Cedar Loop Trail, and Main Trail heading southwest. Then turn right onto paved Cherry Hill Road, cross the tracks, and pick up a trail on the left side of the railroad tracks, soon veering left into the woods. The trail will pass by Wadsworth Falls.

Continue on this single-track trail until it comes out at the tracks again. Cross the railroad bed and pick up the trail on the other side, veering right immediately, then left onto the Main Trail. For a more technical ride, turn left onto the Little Falls Trail, which comes out on the Main Trail. Follow the Main Trail back to the parking area.

# Eastern Connecticut

## RIDE 47  *COCKAPONSET STATE FOREST*

You can ride for an entire day in this large 15,000-acre forest with at least 20 miles of trails and unpaved roads. The fairly challenging 10-mile ride here heads north from Pattaconk Lake, a local recreational area, on technical single-track trails. Then it switches to a two-wheel-drive dirt road, a double-track trail, a jeep road, and more single-track trails. You can then loop back on old asphalt Filley Road, or take dirt roads and trails that fan off it.

The trails are usually dry, and there several stream crossings, which can be rocky. The trails just west of Pattaconk Lake are the most technical ones, while others are mostly flat double-track.

Cockaponset State Forest, named after a Native American chief, is the second-largest state forest in Connecticut. It is a huge woodscape of dark green pines, mountain laurel bushes, and broadleaf trees, including oaks, maples, and dogwoods.

The Pattaconk Lake Recreation Area at the trailhead is a popular site for swimming, sunbathing, and picnicking.

**General location:** The towns of Haddam and Chester, just off Connecticut Highway 9, 12 miles south of Middletown.

**Elevation change:** You will do some steady, not-too-steep climbing on dirt roads and short, steeper rolling on single-track trails.

**Seasons:** Any time between late spring and late fall is good.

**Services:** There are no services in the forest, except for the campgrounds. Exit 3 off CT 9 in Essex has food, shops, and gas. Clark Cycles is located next to the highway. All other services are available in Middletown.

**Hazards:** Watch for minor obstructions on the single-track trails—debris, rocks, and logs. On the two-wheel-drive roads, watch for the occasional vehicle, especially on summer and fall weekends. Since this is a fairly large forest, it's possible to get lost; give yourself plenty of time before dusk.

**Rescue index:** At most you will be about 2 miles from assistance.

**Land status:** State forest trails and roads.

**Maps:** Trail maps may be available at the forest headquarters, located at the northern border of the forest off Exit 8 on CT 9. You can also contact the Bureau of Outdoor Recreation in the Department of Environmental Protection (see Appendix). Many smaller trails are not shown on the official map.

**Finding the trail:** Take Exit 6 on CT 9, onto CT 148 west. After about 1.5 miles, watch for a large lake next to the highway on the right. Turn right just after it, onto Cedar Lake Road. After another 1.5 miles, make a sharp left turn at a sign for Pattaconk Lake. Pass the lake on the right and reach a large parking area on the right.

**Sources of additional information:** Bureau of Outdoor Recreation, Department of Environmental Protection (see Appendix).

**Notes on the trail:** The numerals 4 through 15 on the map indicate the approximate locations of markers at some key trail junctions. To head north, first ride south uphill from the parking lot and turn right onto the first dirt road. There is some logging for about a half mile. This trail heads north, paralleling the blue-blazed Cockaponset and Pattaconk trails, and is at times blazed yellow. (*Note:* Avoid riding on the Cockaponset Trail between Old County Road and Pattaconk Lake. This trail is part of the blue-blazed trail system across Connecticut and is off-limits to cycling in its single-track sections, as of this writing.)

After about 3 miles, you will intersect unpaved Old County Road. Turn left on it, pass a pond on the right, and immediately after the pond, turn right on a jeep road. When this four-wheel-drive path intersects a two-wheel-drive road, turn right onto this unpaved road, Jericho Road.

Now you can loop northward on one of several trails that fork off Jericho Road to the north, and then loop back toward the road. Afterward, head south on patchy but smooth-textured asphalt Filley Road. You can turn off this road to the left toward scenic Turkey Hill Reservoir or pick up Old County Road again on the right, and turn onto double- and single-track trails heading south. Farther down Filley Road, several more trails fork off on the right, heading toward Pattaconk Lake and the parking lot.

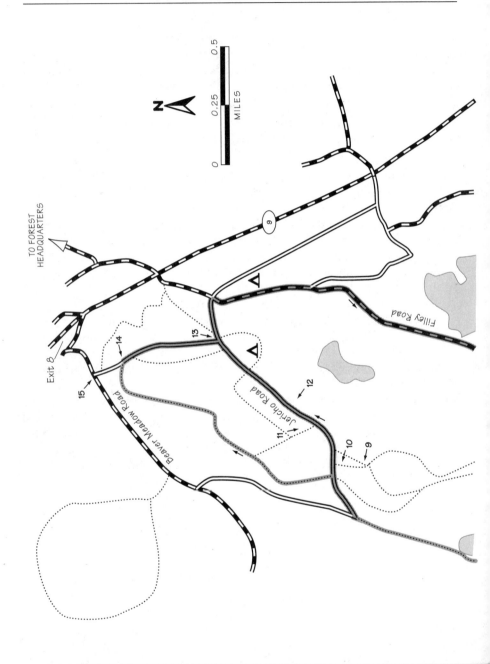

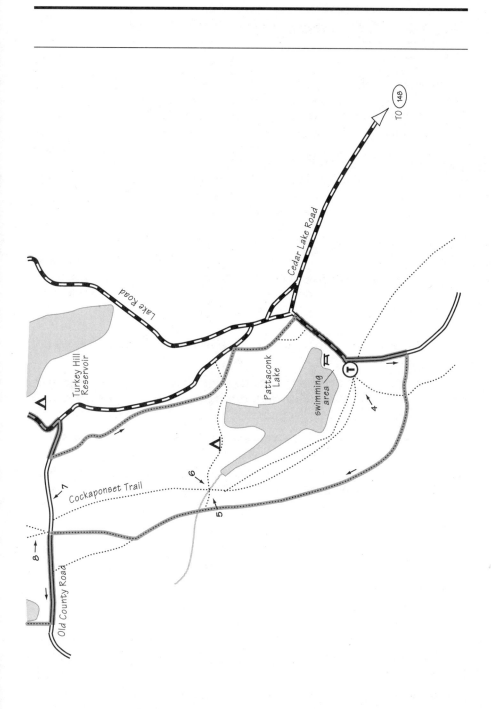

# RIDE 48 *MESHOMASIC STATE FOREST*

This moderately challenging 10-mile loop ride starts on rugged single-track trails for several miles, picks up a jeep road, and finishes up on two-wheel-drive dirt roads. The trails require some technical skill, and the dirt roads will test your climbing ability, but neither terrain is too demanding.

For less-technical riding, you can explore the dirt roads, which crisscross this oldest state forest (1903) in Connecticut. On the secluded single-track trails, you will be immersed in deep woods, with mature hardwood trees (ash, beech, and maple) and bushes brushing up against you.

From the paved access road (Clark Hill Road), you can also reach Great Hill Pond, a local scenic spot. The pond has a foot trail around it that climbs to Great Hill Lookout, a granite outcropping.

This large forest—about 8,000 acres—stretches from north of Connecticut Highway 2 in Glastonbury to south of Clark Hill Road. In between, you'll find miles of trails of various types and degrees of difficulty. Since it's an under-used resource, be prepared for secluded riding.

**General location:** About 10 miles southeast of Hartford and 8 miles east of Middletown, just off CT 2.

**Elevation change:** The ride has a short, steep climb at the beginning, then regular climbing and descending, with shorter climbs on the trails and longer ones on the roads.

**Seasons:** Any time between late spring and late fall is good. Expect some mud in the spring and after a rainfall.

**Services:** All services are available in Middletown (8 miles west) and Glastonbury (5 miles north), including Pig Iron Bike Shop in Glastonbury.

**Hazards:** Watch out for minor obstructions on the trails and an occasional vehicle on the roads. Since this is a large forest, carry plenty of water, food, and repair needs on longer rides.

**Rescue index:** At most you will be about 2.5 miles from assistance.

**Land status:** State forest roads and trails.

**Maps:** *The Connecticut Walk Book,* now in its eighteenth edition, is a map book of trails, including a section for this forest. It is available from the Connecticut Forest and Parks Association, a private, nonprofit organization (see Appendix). As is often the case, some of the trails in this forest are not published.

**Finding the trail:** On CT 2, take Exit 13 onto CT 66 toward East Hampton. In East Hampton turn right onto North Main Street and, after just under a mile,

# RIDE 48 *MESHOMASIC STATE FOREST*

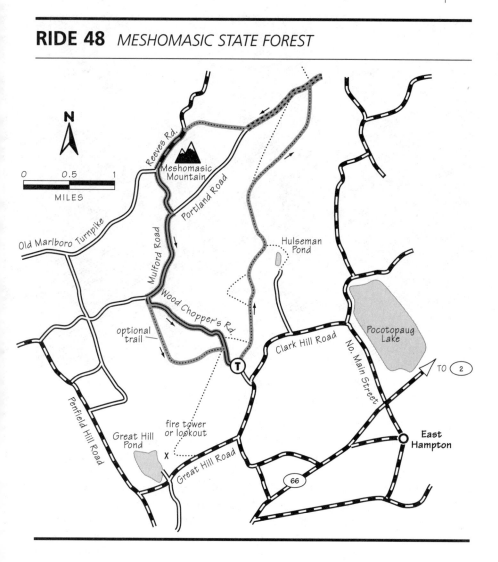

turn left onto Clark Hill Road. After 1.5 miles, turn right onto a two-wheel-drive dirt road with a state forest sign at it. After about a half mile, you reach a parking area on the right, where a blue-dashed trail crosses the road.

**Sources of additional information:** Bureau of Outdoor Recreation, Department of Environmental Protection (see Appendix).

**Notes on the trail:** This is just one possible ride in a large forest. *Note:* The first half of the ride weaves on and off the blue-dashed Shenipsit Trail. Single-track blue-dashed trails are generally not open for biking in Connecticut. However, this policy is open to the discretion of local park rangers.

Expert riders pacing each other. Meshomasic State Forest, East Hampton, Connecticut.

To orient yourself, keep heading north for the first 4 miles. First, though, from the parking area, ride back down the road you came up for less than a half mile and turn left onto a double-track trail into the woods. Fork right after a half mile, picking up the blue-dashed trail. Then fork right off the blue-dashed trail onto another trail (at just under a mile from the beginning of the ride).

At a four-way intersection, turn sharply left, picking up the blue-dashed trail again, then veer to the right on it. At a T junction just west of Hulseman Pond, turn left. Then fork right again off the blue-dashed trail, onto another single-track trail. (You can also continue on the blue-dashed trail.) This unmarked trail comes out on gravel Portland Road.

Turn left on the road and, while descending, turn right sharply onto a double-track trail. (You can also continue on Portland Road.) Keep descending and veering to the right on this trail, and after a steep downhill, you reach a small clearing. Veer left through it and you'll come out on Mulford Road. Then turn left again at the next intersection onto Wood Chopper's Road.

For more trail riding, watch for a double-track trail turning off Wood Chopper's Road on the right soon after the junction with Mulford Road. This trail eventually forks left and comes out near the parking area. Otherwise, after about 1.5 miles on Wood Chopper's Road, you will reach the trailhead on the left.

# RIDE 49 *SHENIPSIT STATE FOREST*

This large, heavily wooded forest (6,200 acres) is a favorite local riding spot. You might find cyclists at the trailhead or around Soapstone Mountain on any weekend. Here's a challenging 12-mile ride using a dozen or so single-track trails, with a return stretch on two secluded woods roads, ending at a lookout tower on Soapstone Mountain just above the trailhead. About 2 miles of the ride are on dirt roads.

This is rolling terrain, with only a moderate amount of climbing—but plenty of loose rock and minor obstructions in some places. The main challenge in this forest is staying oriented on trails that weave south for several miles before turning north. A compass will help—and don't hesitate to ask other bikers for advice.

Soapstone Mountain, with a lookout, is named after the soft rock quarried here until 1888. (There's a nearby foot trail to the quarry.) The stone was first mined by Native Americans, who left behind stone hatchets and arrowheads.

A piece of historical trivia: The "notch" in the otherwise straight border between Massachusetts and Connecticut was given to Massachusetts in 1804 as compensation for several towns near Shenipsit that seceded from the Colony of Massachusetts in 1734.

**General location:** The town of Somers, 20 miles northeast of Hartford.

**Elevation change:** You begin at 700 feet, climb to 800 feet, descend to 600 feet, then climb to 1,000 feet and descend.

**Seasons:** Any time between late spring and late fall is good. Autumn brings glowing maples and oaks.

**Services:** All services are available in Somers and south in Vernon, including the Cycle Center just off Interstate 84, which offers group rides.

**Hazards:** Watch out for debris on some trails—it can jump up and snap a derailleur. And allow plenty of time if you're unfamiliar with the trails here.

**Rescue index:** At most you will be about 3 miles from assistance on secluded trails.

**Land status:** State forest trails and roads.

**Maps:** Contact the Bureau of Outdoor Recreation (see Appendix). Not all of the trails in the forest are mapped.

**Finding the trail:** On I-84, just east of Hartford, take Exit 63 onto Connecticut Highway 83 north toward South Windsor. After 13 miles, turn right onto

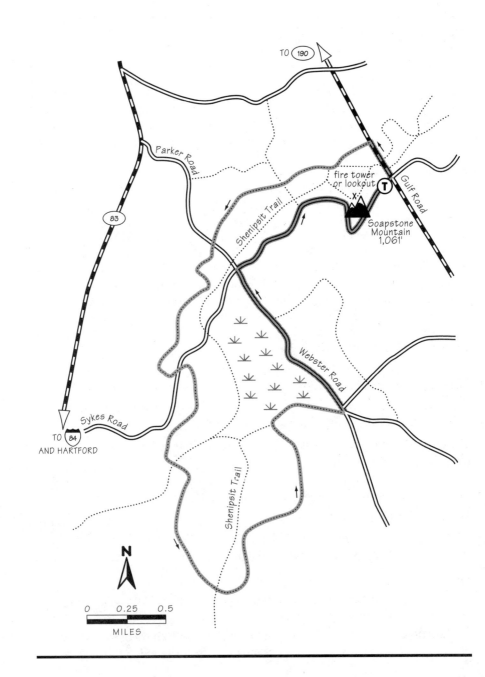

Preparing to ride. Shenipsit State Forest, Somers, Connecticut.

CT 190 in Somers. After another mile, turn right onto Gulf Road, and after about 1 mile, you will reach a paved road on the right that leads up to Soapstone Mountain. Park at the wide turnoffs at the bottom of this road. From the north, take Exit 73 off I-84 onto CT 190 and head west through Stafford. After a couple of miles, turn right onto Gulf Road.

**Sources of additional information:** Bureau of Outdoor Recreation, Department of Environmental Protection (see Appendix), or the Cycle Center in Vernon.

**Notes on the trail:** There are many turns on this 12-mile loop. In particular, it's easy to get disoriented near the southern border. However, the ride stays on clearly defined trails, and many are marked by blue or yellow blazes. Also, you can use dirt Parker, Sykes, and Webster roads to orient yourself. A compass will be helpful.

Ride back northward on paved Gulf Road for a short distance, and turn left into the woods on the second double-track trail along the road, just after a house. (The first trail is the Shenipsit Trail, a blue-blazed hiking trail.) After about a mile, fork left. After another half mile, you will come out on a double-track trail. Veer left (south), and almost immediately fork right, then left again. (You can bail out on the double-track trail by heading straight on it, soon reaching the dirt access road to the lookout tower.)

At 2.3 miles, after a rocky downhill, veer to the right, and you will reach Parker Road. Turn left on the road and take the first double-track trail on the right, staying to the right at the next intersection. You will join a blue-dashed trail and continue climbing. At the next fork, turn right off the blue-dashed trail.

You will cross a second dirt road, Sykes Road (this is about 4 miles into the ride). For a shorter ride, turn left on the road and climb to the lookout tower. Otherwise, cross the road and continue on a single-track trail. At a T junction, turn left, heading south. You will cross a narrow dirt road. Turn left at the next fork, then right onto a blue-dashed trail for a short distance, then fork left onto a narrower double-track trail.

Just before you reach a large logging clearing at the southern end of the forest, turn almost 180 degrees to the left, heading north. You reach a T junction; turn right (toward Webster Road). When you come out on the road, turn left, continue until you intersect Parker Road, turn right on it, and climb to the lookout tower. Take the paved road down from the tower toward the trailhead on Gulf Road.

# RIDE 50 *SCHOOLHOUSE BROOK PARK*

You can fashion a 5-mile loop on both grassy and rocky single- and double-track trails in this well-maintained, wooded park, which is also used by hikers. Its natural attractions include two ponds, Barrow's Pond and Bicentennial Pond; delicate new growth; large moss-covered boulders; and to the northeast, on the Juniper and Tamarack trails, a stretch lined with handsome evergreen trees. This is pleasant, easy mountain biking.

There's also swimming and picnicking at Bicentennial Pond, which has a sandy beach and bathhouse.

As of this writing, biking is allowed on all the trails except for the Fitness Trail and Byron's Trail.

For cultural and social offerings, including eateries and hangouts, there's the large University of Connecticut campus in nearby Storrs.

**General location:** 3 miles south of Storrs, 9 miles south of Interstate 84, and 25 miles east of Hartford.

**Elevation change:** The terrain is relatively flat, with some short hills. A few side trails have more challenging climbs.

**Seasons:** You can ride here year-round, but cyclists are asked to stay off the

# RIDE 50 *SCHOOLHOUSE BROOK PARK*

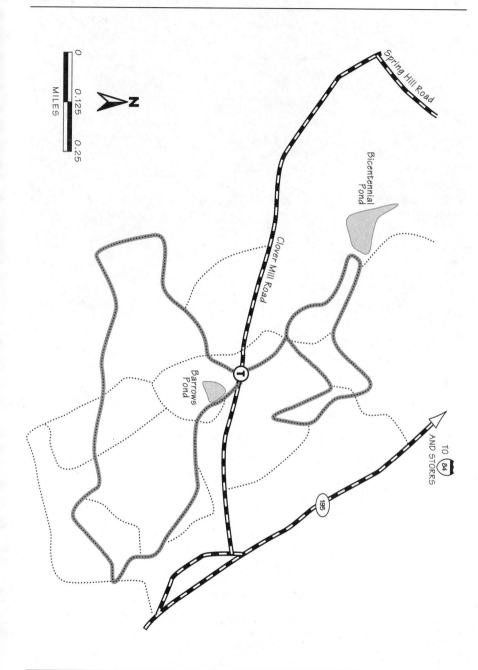

A leaf-covered trail past an old stone wall. Schoolhouse Brook Park, Mansfield, Connecticut.

trails in wet conditions, especially in the spring. During the winter, the trails are used by cross-country skiers; avoid riding across their tracks.

**Services:** All services are available in Storrs and Willimantic.

**Hazards:** In autumn, watch out for minor obstructions, such as loose rocks and logs, which can be hidden underneath the leaves. Slow down around corners to avoid startling other users.

**Rescue index:** At most you will be about a half mile from a traveled road.

**Land status:** Town public trails. Local mountain bikers help to maintain these trails, establish guidelines, and educate bicyclists. The rules for mountain biking are posted on a board at the parking area. They include: yield to pedestrians; walk through muddy areas; respect water bars; don't create turnouts; and limit group rides to five people.

**Maps:** A packet of trail maps is stocked in a box outside the Parks and Recreation Office inside the Town Hall in Storrs, located at the junction of Connecticut Highways 195 and 275.

**Finding the trail:** Take Exit 68 on I-84 and head south on CT 195. After about 8 miles, you reach Storrs. Continue on CT 195, and after around 2.7 miles, turn right sharply onto Clover Mill Road. After a half mile, you reach an unpaved parking lot with a sign on the right.

**Sources of additional information:** Mansfield Parks and Recreation Department (see Appendix).

**Notes on the trail:** Most of the trails are marked with names on wooden signposts ("Oak Ridge," "Bird Loop," "Pine Ridge," etc.). On the trail map, a legend ranks the trails by difficulty for cross-country skiing. About two-thirds of the loops fan out to the left (southeast) of Clover Mill Road, while the others head northwest.

To do a 2.5-mile loop to the southeast, ride across the paved road from the parking lot and veer right onto Stone Bridge Trail (white rectangles). After about a mile, following the white blazings, you will reach the blue-blazed Barrow's Trail. Turn right and continue east. After passing a field on the right, turn sharply left (staying on Barrow's Trail). While climbing, turn right onto Heritage Trail (also white blazes). You will reach secluded Barrow's Pond, near Clover Mill Road.

Several scenic trails interconnect northwest of the parking area. To make a large counterclockwise loop, begin on the Road Runner Trail, turn right onto the Nipmuck Trail, right onto Juniper Trail, and right again onto the Tamarack Trail. Then loop to the left, heading northwest toward Bicentennial Pond, and then south on the Road Runner trails.

# RIDE 51 BLUFF POINT AND HALEY FARM STATE PARKS

Bluff Point State Park has a unique distinction: it's the last remaining major parcel of undeveloped land along the Connecticut coastline. Nearby Haley Farm was featured in *Life* magazine in the 1970s as a victory for conservationists. It's no wonder today they're both popular places for biking and hiking.

Don't be misled by the modest size of these two areas (778 acres and 198 acres). They offer plenty of riding opportunities. At Bluff Point, along with the large loop on old jeep roads, single-track enthusiasts can explore several miles of tight trails in the eastern half of the park. These winding paths were created by the land's first explorers and inhabitants—deer. Scenic trails and roads also follow the coastline at Bluff Point and Bushy Point.

Take some time to relax along the seacoast, and enjoy the beaches, rocky cliffs, and open fields. Bluff Point, which was designated as a "coastal reserve"

# RIDE 51 *BLUFF POINT AND HALEY FARM STATE PARKS*

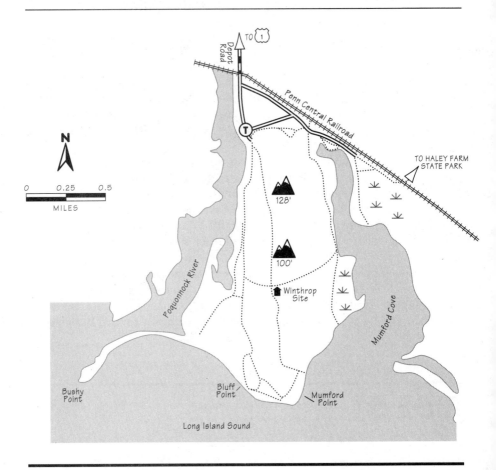

in 1975, is actually made up of both a saltwater marsh and beach landscape and an inner upland ridge. Along the roads and trails near the shore, you can find native beach plum, beach pea, red and white shore roses, sedges, and rushes. Inland, the habitat is a mixed hardwood forest.

In the nineteenth century, the sloping fields at Bluff Point were the front lawns of mansions (one can still see the remnants of orchards), similar to the more-famous Newport, Rhode Island. Now they are grassy fields with trails to be enjoyed by everyone.

Haley Farm was a working seventeenth-century farm. Its owner, Caleb Haley, practiced an unusual hobby: building large stone walls. At times, he used two oxen to pull huge stones out of the ground. Today, the park is a habitat of rolling pastures, freshwater ponds and swamps, and salt marshes.

**General location:** The town of Groton, about 2.5 miles south of U.S. Highway 1 and Interstate 95.

**Elevation change:** Despite its coastal location, there's a climb to 125 feet in Bluff Point, with several trails and roads rising and descending from this high point. Otherwise, it's mostly flat riding.

**Seasons:** This can be a four-season ride, with good drainage on the roads. Avoid the wooded trails in wetter conditions.

**Services:** Restrooms are available in the Bluff Point parking area. All other services are along US 1 and in Groton. Bicycle Barn is on US 1 in Groton near the park.

**Hazards:** Both of these parks are used heavily by cyclists, joggers, and walkers. Ride responsibly on both the well-used roads and the more secluded trails, which have tight, blind turns. Some of the single-track trails in Bluff Point are technical, with plenty of roots and embedded rocks.

**Rescue index:** You will be no more than a half mile from a traveled road or trailhead.

**Land status:** Trails and roads in public parks.

**Maps:** Maps are available at the parking areas. The "official" maps do not show most of the single-track trails.

**Finding the trail:** To Bluff Point State Park: Take Exit 88 off I-95 and head south on Connecticut Highway 117. After 0.8 mile, turn right onto US 1. After 0.2 mile, just after passing a school building on the left, turn left onto Depot Road. After another 0.2 mile, veer right underneath a railroad bridge, and you will reach a large parking lot. To Haley Farm State Park: Head 1.1 miles east on US 1 from the junction of US 1 and CT 117, and fork right onto CT 215. After 0.5 mile, turn right onto Brook Street, and after another 0.5 mile, right onto Haley Farm Lane.

**Sources of additional information:** Fort Griswold State Park or Groton Town Manager (see Appendix).

**Notes on the trail:** At the Bluff Point parking area, you can begin riding on the wide dirt road going due south, along the Pequonnock River. After about a half mile, you can either continue straight to Bluff Point and the coastline, or turn left and climb on a rockier, more rugged trail to the high point. From there, one can turn right on the main loop to the shore, or left for a short distance, and then either left to do a short loop back to the parking area, or straight on a narrow trail to reach several challenging single-track trails on the eastern side of the park.

A seashore singletrack. Bluff Point State Park, Groton, Connecticut.

Be sure to take the singletracks and roads that skirt the coastline at the southern edge of the park for excellent views of the ocean.

To reach Haley Farm State Park, turn left at the parking area onto a shadier dirt road. Follow this road and trails off it as they head southeast, paralleling the railroad tracks. After 1.5 miles, watch for a small, short tunnel underneath the railroad tracks on the right. This connecting trail will reach Haley Farm. The railroad company is planning to build a pedestrian/biking bridge over the tracks connecting the parks, as well as constructing a fence between the trails and tracks, sometime around 2000.

# RIDE 52  *JAMES L. GOODWIN STATE FOREST*

One can do either easy or more challenging rides in this well-maintained, conservation-oriented forest. Beginning at a large pond, lawn, or tree farm, choose either dirt roads, double-track trails, a rail-trail, or more challenging single-track trails. (The rangers ask that cyclists not use a few of the narrower trails, especially around the ponds.)

James Goodwin, Connecticut's most famous conservationist, donated these 2,200 acres to the state. In 1913, he wrote: "One has only to look at the abundance of picturesque hills and valleys and streams in the state, once thickly covered with dense forest where Indians roamed, and now rapidly becoming despoiled of their freshness, to realize that there exist few more attractive and at the same time more accessible spots than we have in Connecticut." Ride on.

Some stretches of single-track trails here are rock-strewn, requiring good bike-handling skills. To the north, the loop enters Natchaug State Forest (see Ride 53). For easier riding, there's a rail-trail connecting the two forests.

**General location:** Town of Hampton, just north of U.S. Highway 6.

**Elevation change:** There's a moderately steep half-mile climb from Morey Road to Kingsbury Road; the rest of the ride is relatively flat, with some regular short hills.

**Seasons:** This can be a four-season ride, with shade in the summer and colorful foliage in October and November. Avoid crossing ski-touring tracks in the winter.

**Services:** All services are available in Willimantic and on US 6.

**Hazards:** Some of the single-track trails on the first 3 miles are covered with rocks and other minor obstructions.

**Rescue index:** At most you will be about 1 mile from assistance on secluded trails.

# RIDE 52 *JAMES L. GOODWIN STATE FOREST*

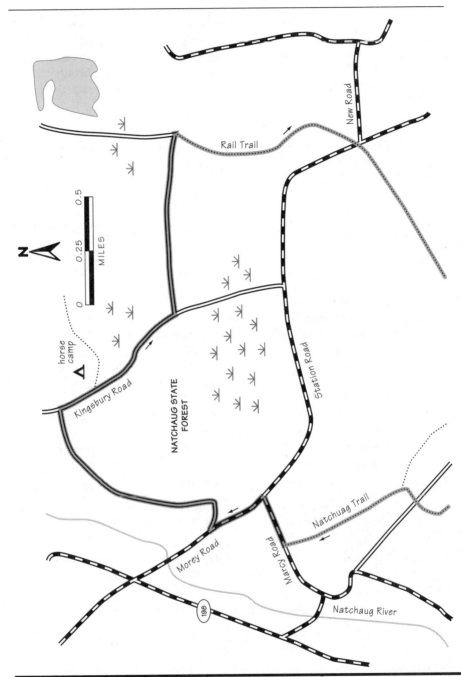

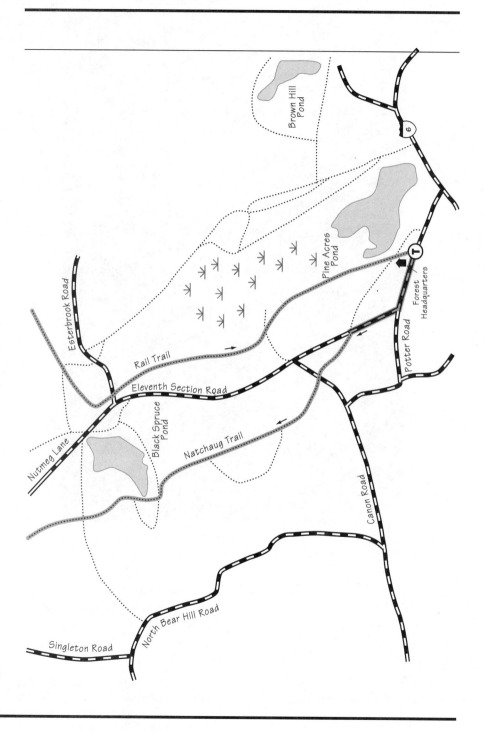

A narrow trail in deep woods. James L. Goodwin State Forest, Hampton, Connecticut.

**Land status:** State forest trails and woods roads. Blue-blazed hiking trails, found throughout Connecticut, are not officially open for mountain biking. However, specific policies are established by local rangers.

**Maps:** A trail map may be available at the forest headquarters. Or contact the Bureau of Outdoor Recreation (see Appendix).

**Finding the trail:** On US 6, follow the brown state forest signs. The access road, Potter Road, is 1.2 miles west of the junction of Connecticut Highway 97 and

US 6. Drive up the access road to a parking area on the right, across from the headquarters building.

**Sources of additional information:** James L. Goodwin State Forest (see Appendix).

**Notes on the trail:** It is relatively easy to stay oriented in the park, with several distinct kinds of riding terrain. The route on the map shows one 9-mile loop, beginning at forest headquarters, using Potter Road to reach the Natchaug Trail heading northward. On the trail, you cross unpaved Nutmeg Lane. Dogleg to the left and right, picking up another gated woods road. You will reach a clearing and turn left, passing through an opening in a stone wall. Follow the blue blazes until you come out on paved Marcy Road.

Turn right on the pavement and left at the next intersection, onto paved Morey Road (or right to shorten the ride). While descending on Morey Road, turn sharply right onto an unpaved woods road. Climb and reach a T junction with Kingsbury Road in Natchaug State Forest. Then the loop turns southward on the rail-trail.

Some trails are also open on the eastern side of the forest nearer Brown Hill Pond; drop in at the headquarters for more information.

# RIDE 53 *NATCHAUG STATE FOREST*

You can ride vigorously on the 7 miles of secluded woods roads in this 12,500-acre forest or cruise along and take in the scenery: deciduous trees that turn bright orange and red in autumn, giant evergreens, marsh land, a river, and a lake.

Smooth dirt and gravel roads make up most of this moderate loop ride, with an optional 1.5-mile shortcut on a more rugged double-track trail and about a mile on old asphalt. On the paved stretch at the end of the loop, you might stop at a scenic picnic and recreational area along the Natchaug River, with groves of hemlock trees.

The marsh land on the eastern edge of the forest is a favorite bird-watching site, as well as a place for spotting other wildlife—if you're quiet. On the northern edge of the ride, you pass a quail farm. This ride can be linked with the James L. Goodwin State Forest ride (see Ride 52).

**General location:** Just off Connecticut Highway 198, between U.S. Highway 44 and US 6.

**Elevation change:** In a counterclockwise direction, you begin by climbing gently and steadily for about a mile, then rolling for about 4 miles, and finally climbing fairly steeply on pavement for the last 1.5 miles.

# RIDE 53 *NATCHAUG STATE FOREST*

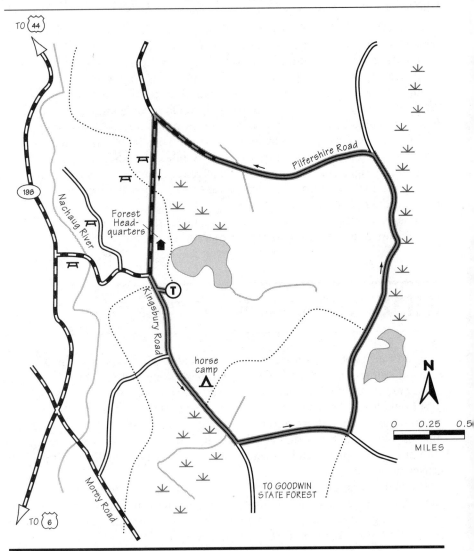

**Seasons:** This can be a four-season ride. It is well drained in the spring, shady in the summer, colorful in the fall, and secluded in the winter.

**Services:** All services are available in Willimantic. There's camping at several campgrounds along CT 198.

**Hazards:** None, except for occasional horseback riders (yield to them) and motorized vehicles on the roads.

Cruising through a forest. Natchaug State Forest, Eastford, Connecticut.

**Rescue index:** At most you will be about 2 miles from assistance.

**Land status:** State forest roads and trails.

**Maps:** Maps are available from the Bureau of Outdoor Recreation (see Appendix).

**Finding the trail:** From the north on US 44, turn south onto CT 198. You reach the forest entrance on the left after about 3 miles. From the south on US 6, turn north onto CT 198, then right at a small brown sign for the state forest. Climb an asphalt access road until you reach a T junction, after 0.7 mile. Turn right onto a dirt road and almost immediately left onto another dirt road (toward the Beaver Dam Wildlife Management Area). You will reach a parking area almost immediately.

**Sources of additional information:** The contact for this forest is at nearby Mashamoquet State Park (see Appendix) or the Department of Environmental Protection Eastern District Headquarters (see Appendix).

**Notes on the trail:** This ride is easy to follow: turn left at all major intersections (with an optional shortcut on a trail). First ride south on unpaved Kingsbury Road, fork left, and left again, passing a reservoir on the right. (To do the shortcut on a trail, turn left onto a narrow dirt road just under 1 mile from the beginning of the ride. You'll soon reach a fork. To the left is the Silvermine Horse Camp area; to the right, a trail enters the woods, rejoining the other side of the loop.)

Otherwise, continue on Kingsbury Road, making two sharp left turns; you'll be heading north. (Turning right at any of the preceding forks will bring you to the James L. Goodwin State Forest, Ride 52.) Fork left again, onto unpaved Pilfershire Road, which crosses a brook, becomes paved, and climbs. When it levels off, turn left sharply on another paved road. You will pass a large picnic area along the river on the right and several forest headquarters buildings. Ride through the junction where you came into the forest, then turn left to reach the parking area.

# RIDE 54 *PACHAUG STATE FOREST*

At 24,000 acres, this largest forest in Connecticut has some of the most scenic and convenient woods-road and trail riding in southern New England, including about 20 miles of single-track trails. It's worth a trip to this less-settled part of the state to explore these secluded, sunny roads and winding trails. Afterward, you can relax at one of many picnic sites, take a short hike to a lookout, or just stretch out at secluded Phillips Pond or busier Beachdale Pond.

This moderate 9-mile loop explores the central section of the forest, using a network of smooth, narrow, secluded dirt roads, a double-track trail, and three optional stretches on single-track trails. It's just a sampling of the many possible rides here on connecting trails and roads. More trails lie in the section of the forest east of Connecticut Highway 49.

**General location:** In the southeastern corner of Connecticut, just off Interstate 395 and about 15 miles east of Norwich.

**Elevation change:** The roads and trails in the forest are flat or rolling, with an occasional moderate climb.

**Seasons:** If there is little snow, this can be a four-season ride. Avoid riding on the trails in wet conditions.

**Services:** Water and restrooms are available at the trailhead and Phillips Pond. First-come, first-serve campsites are located at Mt. Misery. All other services are available along CT 138 and in Norwich.

A woods-road with trailheads. Pachaug State Forest, Pachaug, Connecticut.

**Hazards:** Watch for occasional motorized traffic on the roads, especially on summer weekends. Be considerate of hikers and horseback riders. If you decide to explore the forest on your own, be aware that this is a huge area—although it's divided into several large sections—and many of the trails are blazed with the same blue markings.

**Rescue index:** At most you will be about 1.5 miles from assistance.

**Land status:** Roads and trails in a public forest.

**Maps:** The Bureau of Outdoor Recreation (see Appendix) has a map of the dirt roads and a few trails. Many of the single-track trails in this forest are unmapped.

**Finding the trail:** On I-395 take Exit 85, and head east on CT 138. After several miles, turn left (north) onto CT 49. (From nearby Rhode Island, you can take either Rhode Island Highway 138 west or RI 165 west.) After about a half mile on CT 49, you will see a small, brown state forest sign on the left at the forest access road. Turn left onto this paved road. You can park at a lot near CT 49 or drive up the access road for 0.7 mile to a large parking area on the left.

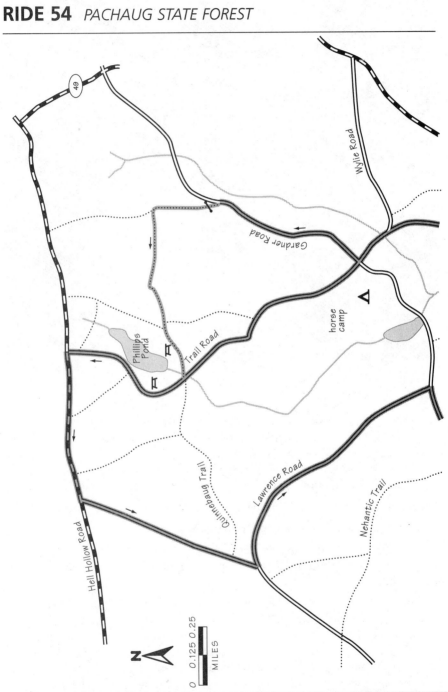

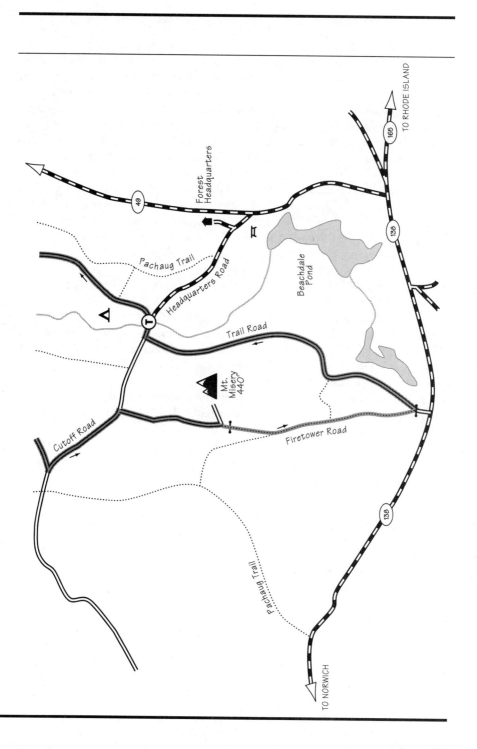

**Sources of additional information:** Pachaug State Forest (see Appendix).

**Notes on the trail:** There are two distinct kinds of riding in this forest: dirt roads and trails. This 9-mile loop uses mainly dirt roads, with three single-track options. You can do shorter rides by looping back toward the parking area at several junctions, or longer ones by taking connecting roads and trails.

Begin by heading north from the camping area on Trail Road. Continue through two intersections, past Phillips Pond, and come out on paved Hell Hollow Road. Turn left and pick up the next dirt road to the left. At the next intersection, turn left onto dirt Lawrence Road, right at the next intersection, then left onto Cutoff Road.

Now you can ride back to the trailhead or turn right onto Firetower Road, which passes the trailhead for Mt. Misery, then becomes a gated double-track trail. When this trail reaches a gate at the southern edge of the forest, turn sharply left onto Trail Road, which heads back to the parking area.

*Three trail-riding options:* Begin on the blue-blazed Pachaug Trail, which forks off the paved access road a short distance from CT 49. This trail comes out on Wylie Road. Turn left and right onto Trail Road. (The Pachaug Trail north of Wylie Road is not passable.)

At the next four-way intersection, turn right onto Gardner Road and, after about a mile, you will pass a gated double-track trail on the left. Turn onto it, and at the next intersection turn left onto another double-track trail, then right at the next intersection. You will come out at Phillips Pond. (There are more interconnecting trails in this area.)

Just west of the pond, you can pick up the Quinnebaug Trail, which winds west, coming out on a dirt road near Lawrence Road. More trails wind south from there toward Firetower Road.

# RHODE ISLAND

# RIDE 55  *GREAT SWAMP MANAGEMENT AREA*

This 6-mile ride explores a wetland on several scenic, grassy roads that turn into double-track trails. You can crank along at a fast pace—but you'll miss the scenery and wildlife. About a third of the ride skirts a large wetland, where you might spy waterfowl nesting. In the autumn, maples and other deciduous trees show their colors.

There's an out-and-back side trail to the grassy shoreline of a large pond and an inner loop that climbs to a modest view.

If you're a newcomer to Rhode Island, you might also visit the small, yet bustling, city of Newport (Rhode Island Highway 138 to the east), with its public beaches, historic mansions, seafood restaurants, world-famous folk and jazz festivals, and scenic road-riding along the coast.

**General location:** At the junction of RI 2 and RI 138, 5 miles west of Kingston.

**Elevation change:** The ride is relatively flat, with one short climb possible.

**Seasons:** Spring and fall are the best seasons for riding, with good drainage in the spring and colorful foliage in autumn. Late fall is hunting season—see Hazards.

**Services:** All services are available to the east in Kingston. Two bike shops: Stedmans on Main Street in Wakefield and King's Cyclery on Post Road in Westerly.

**Hazards:** Great Swamp is a popular hunting site from around mid-October through December. The rangers suggest that mountain bicyclists wear orange during this time. Call or check at the management area headquarters for hunting dates (see Appendix).

**Rescue index:** You will be about 1 mile from assistance on easily traversed terrain.

**Land status:** Roads in a public management area.

**Maps:** A map and other information are available at the headquarters.

**Finding the trail:** Take Exit 3A on Interstate 95 onto RI 138 toward Kingston and Newport. From Providence, take RI 2 to RI 138 and turn left. After about 8 miles, cross RI 2 and continue until you pass a sign on the right for the Great Swamp Management Area, just before the junction with RI 110. Turn right and follow this road. It becomes unpaved, passes a cluster of Division of Fish and Wildlife headquarters buildings on the right, enters the management area, and arrives at an unpaved parking lot.

**Sources of additional information:** Great Swamp Management Area or Division of Fish and Wildlife, Department of Environmental Management (see Appendix).

# RIDE 55 *GREAT SWAMP MANAGEMENT AREA*

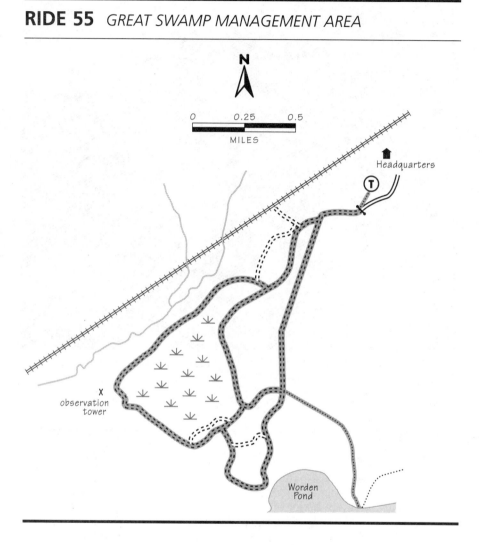

**Notes on the trail:** This ride is easy to follow. To do the large loop, fork right after just under a half mile, then right again at 1 mile. Follow the trail as it winds around the wetland. After passing the shoreline of the "swamp," you will reach another fork. Take the left fork for a shorter, elevated trail back to the trailhead. Otherwise, fork right. You will reach a three-way intersection. Turn right for a half-mile side trip to Worden Pond. Otherwise, fork left and head back to the parking area. Then loop around again, exploring the paths you missed the first time.

Cruising around a wetland. Great Swamp Management Area, Kingston, Rhode Island.

# RIDE 56 *ARCADIA MANAGEMENT AREA*

This popular mountain biking site in central Rhode Island draws riders to its 30 miles of secluded single-track trails. For those seeking less-technical riding, several miles of quiet, secluded dirt roads crisscross in this 10,000-acre forest. (This area is also used by hikers. To avoid startling and alienating them, slow down and announce your presence in a friendly way.)

The fairly challenging 12-mile ride in this book follows a perimeter loop on mainly single-track trails, winding through a highly diverse landscape of large pine trees, smaller hardwoods, mountain laurel and other bushes, ferns and grasses, a large pond, and streams. In the center of the area lies Breakheart Pond, a pleasant place for a break.

There are more trails south of Rhode Island Highway 165. Four miles east of Arcadia on RI 165, there's a sandy beach at a huge pond straddling the Rhode Island–Connecticut border.

**General location:** A few miles west of Interstate 95, 25 miles southwest of Providence.

**Elevation change:** Although the area is relatively flat, many single-track trails roll up and down. The roads are flatter.

**Seasons:** This can be a four-season ride. Note: Do not ride on the trails during wet conditions.

**Services:** Be sure to bring plenty of water, since there is none in the management area. All services are available along RI 102 and RI 3, and in Hope Valley to the south.

**Hazards:** Watch for horseback riders and hikers. If you ride during the hunting season, from around late November through December, wear bright clothing. Check with the area manager for hunting dates (see Appendix).

**Rescue index:** At most you will be about 2 miles from assistance on secluded trails.

**Land status:** Old roads and trails on public land.

**Maps:** The Department of Environmental Management has a rough trail map (see Appendix).

**Finding the trail:** Take Exit 5A on I-95, onto RI 102 south. Veer right onto RI 3 south (following signs for RI 165). Turn right at a blinking light onto RI 165 west. After about 2.5 miles, you will reach a small, white church on the right. You can park at the church—*except for Sunday mornings*—or turn right after the church and park in a parking area.

**Sources of additional information:** Arcadia Management Area (see Appendix).

**Notes on the trail:** You can do at least two completely different rides here: an intricate loop on single-track trails or a less technical, simpler ride on dirt roads (or a combination of them). The 12-mile ride described below uses quite a few trails. Almost the entire ride should be blazed with yellow dots—and white and orange dots on two trails at the end.

Here's a turn-by-turn description of this counterclockwise loop. Ride east on RI 165 for about 0.3 mile, and turn left into the management area on a four-wheel-drive road, soon passing a board with a sign, "John B. Hudson Trail, 1.6 miles." A large map of the area is located here, as well as a box that may contain trail maps. (A few hundred feet farther on this trail, you can take a short side trail on the left to a small observation tower.)

When you reach a narrow dirt road, turn right on it, then almost immediately fork left onto the John B. Hudson Trail at a double yellow blazing. At a small clearing, this single-track trail blends into a wider trail. Continue in the same direction (north), and you will reach Breakheart Pond.

Turn right on the dirt road in front of the pond, pass through a gate, and almost immediately turn left at the yellow blazes. After a few hundred feet, fork left where a sign tells distances and directions to several destinations.

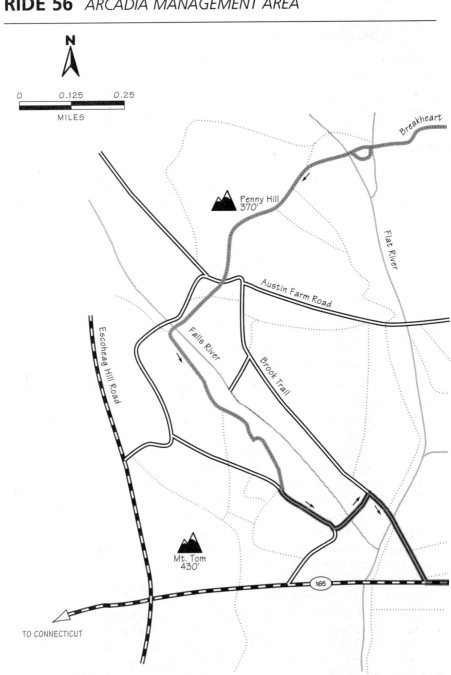

N

| 0 | 0.125 | 0.25 |

MILES

Breakheart

Penny Hill
370'

Flat River

Austin Farm Road

Falls River

Brook Trail

Escoheag Hill Road

Mt. Tom
430'

165

TO CONNECTICUT

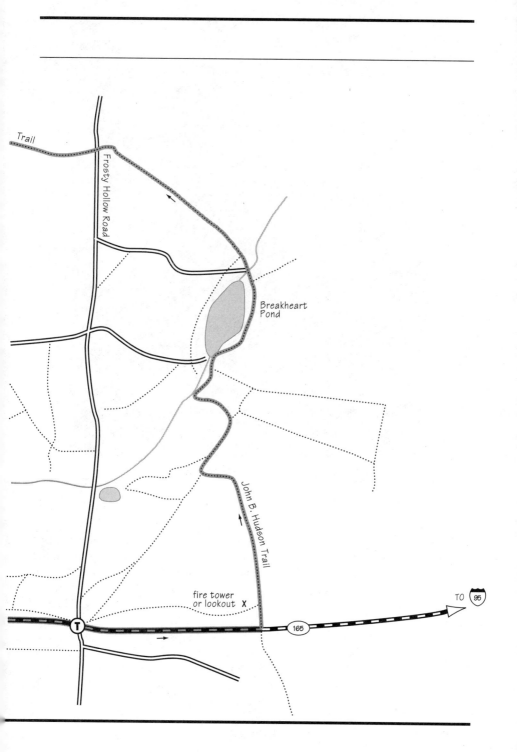

Trail

Frosty Hollow Road

Breakheart
Pond

John B. Hudson Trail

fire tower
or lookout **X**

165

TO 95

Serious single-tracking. Arcadia Management Area, Hope Valley, Rhode Island.

Soon you will cross a bridge. Keep right at a fork, although both trail options link up later. You will come out on a wider trail and veer right (following the yellow blazes). When you reach a T junction with a wider trail, turn left and cross a small wooden bridge. When you pass several large boulders on the right, turn right at a white arrow and a sign for the Breakheart Trail, which is what you want.

Go through a four-way intersection of trails, cross a dirt road, and make a dogleg turn to the right and left to pick up the yellow-blazed Breakheart Trail again. Go straight at the next intersection (yellow blazes). Then turn right at an intersection with a wider trail, cross a bridge, and fork left after it. Turn left at the next fork.

You will reach Penny Hill, which offers a modest view through pine trees. Continue riding southwest, cross dirt Austin Farm Road, veer right onto another narrow dirt road, and almost immediately turn left at the yellow blazes. You come out onto a two-wheel-drive road. Turn left and cross a bridge. Almost immediately fork left onto a white-blazed trail, the Escoheag Trail. At the next fork, turn left onto the Sand Hill Trail, which is marked with orange blazes. This trail comes out on a dirt road. Turn left, pass through a gate, reach a T junction, turn left again, and cross a wooden bridge. At the next T junction, turn right and cruise down to RI 165. Turn left to return to the parking lot.

# RIDE 57 *NEW LONDON TURNPIKE*

This unpaved road—a major thoroughfare in a bygone era—makes a pleasant, secluded out-and-back ride. The 7-mile road alternates between smooth, rolling two-wheel-drive stretches past fields and farms, stone walls, ponds, and occasional homes—and four-wheel-drive sections that will keep you focused on loose gravel, embedded rock, and occasional dips. The "turnpike" bisects a state-managed area with an extensive network of single-track trails (Ride 58).

**General location:** Near Interstate 95, from West Warwick to Exeter.

**Elevation change:** Relatively flat, with gradual climbs and descents.

**Seasons:** This can be a four-season ride.

**Services:** All services are available along Rhode Island Highway 3, including Valley Mountain Bikes in West Warwick.

**Hazards:** None, except for the occasional traffic at the crossroads.

**Rescue index:** At most you will be about a half mile from assistance.

**Land status:** Public town roads.

**Maps:** Any detailed state road map will show the turnpike. The state offers an excellent free state map. (see Appendix).

**Finding the trail:** Take Exit 7 (Coventry/West Warwick) on Interstate 95. Turn right immediately and you will reach a large commuter parking area on the right, where you can park. Continue riding up the road for a short distance and you will reach a gated dirt road—this is the northern end of the turnpike.

**Sources of additional information:** Planning and Development, Department of Environmental Management, or Rhode Island Tourism Bureau (see Appendix).

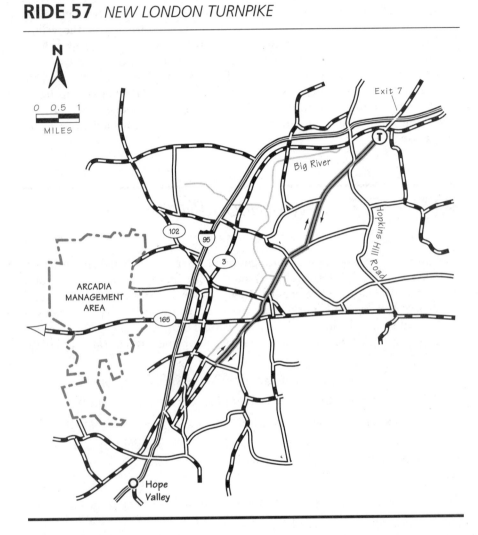

**Notes on the trail:** After riding southward for around 7 miles, you will reach an intersection with a small waterfall on the right side. The "turnpike" becomes a paved road south of this junction. You can also loop back on scenic roads to the east. For more technical riding, explore the single-track trails that intersect the turnpike near its northern end (Ride 58).

# RIDE 58 *BIG RIVER MANAGEMENT AREA*

This area is laced with single-track trails, as well as several secluded dirt roads. Many of these rolling, twisting trails were made years ago by motorized dirt bikes. Today, local mountain bikers use them to hone their cornering skills. It's a pleasant, quiet environment, with pine needles carpeting some trails.

This 10-mile ride (made up of several smaller loops) begins and ends on a half-mile stretch of old road. About a mile of the ride also uses double-track trails. The rest of the time, you're weaving in the woods on narrow trails, with plenty of roots and rock, and an occasional mud hole. Although the trails are in relatively good condition, some inclines are eroded, with lots of loose rock and dirt.

You can make shorter loops, too, or do less-technical riding on the jeep roads that intersect this pine and shrub forest (Ride 57).

**General location:** Just off Exit 6 on Interstate 95, about 20 miles south of Providence.

**Elevation change:** Although the area is flat overall, the trails roll up and down—not unlike an amusement park ride.

**Seasons:** Any time between late spring and late fall is good. Local cyclists ride here year-round, although late fall to early winter is hunting season. Check with the Department of Environmental Management about hunting dates (see Appendix).

**Services:** All services are available on Rhode Island Highway 3 and in Coventry.

**Hazards:** These tight single-track trails require concentration. Around a corner, a steep, eroded downhill section may await, demanding good bike-handling and braking skills. Also, because this is a secluded area, you might consider carrying a compass to stay oriented.

**Rescue index:** At most, you will be a couple of miles from assistance on secluded trails.

**Land status:** Trails and old roads through land managed by the state Department of Environmental Management (see Appendix)

**Maps:** A detailed state road map will show the roads that intersect and border this unmapped area.

**Finding the trail:** Take Exit 6 on I-95, onto RI 3 toward West Greenwich. Within a hundred yards or so, a small paved parking area will come up on the left, next to the trailhead and Burnt Sawmill Road. Or, drive up the old asphalt access road to a small parking area.

# RIDE 58 *BIG RIVER MANAGEMENT AREA*

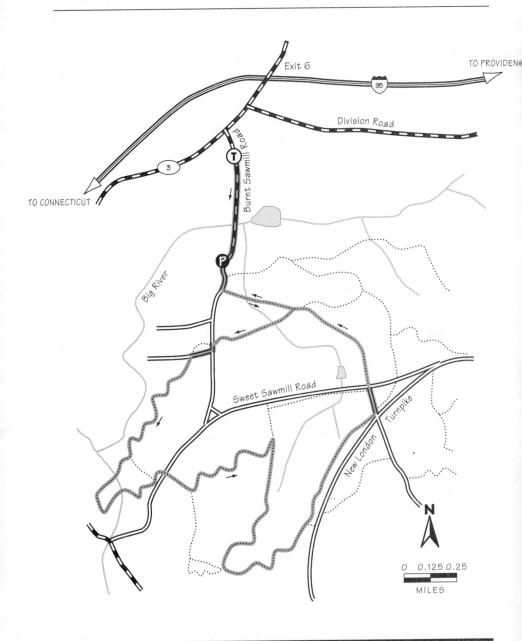

Exit 6

TO PROVIDEN

95

Division Road

Burnt Sawmill Road

3

TO CONNECTICUT

T

P

Big River

Sweet Sawmill Road

New London Turnpike

N

0   0.125  0.25

MILES

**Sources of additional information:** Division of Fish and Wildlife, Department of Environmental Management (see Appendix).

**Notes on the trail:** This area is full of trails winding through deep woods. You can use the three dirt roads in it to stay oriented—you might cruise on them first to get a feel for the layout of the land. This map shows four interconnecting "loops," which will take you progressively farther away from the trailhead. You can follow any of these loops. The trails on them should be well-trodden—if you find yourself on an overgrown trail, turn around and take the more-traveled one.

*Loop 1:* Begin by riding up old asphalt Burnt Sawmill Road, which turns to dirt after a half mile. Almost immediately after it becomes unpaved, turn left onto a double-track trail at a telephone pole. Stay on this main double-track trail, and you will soon reach a T junction at a wider double-track trail. Turn right and you will reach another T junction with Burnt Sawmill Road; turn left. If you look to the right, you should be able to see a gate across the road. (For a short ride, you can turn right to return to the trailhead.)

*Loop 2:* After turning left onto Burnt Sawmill Road, climb for a short distance and fork right onto a narrow dirt road. After about a hundred feet, turn left onto a single-track trail. Stay on this trail, bearing right, and then forking right. (For a shorter loop, fork left; you will come out on the same dirt road you reach later.) Fork left at the next intersection, bear left again, and you will emerge at a four-way intersection.

Go straight across this intersection, onto a single-track trail. You will reach another four-way intersection. This is Sweet Sawmill Road. Go straight across it onto a narrow dirt road. (For a shorter ride, turn left on the dirt road.)

*Loop 3:* After a short distance, fork left onto a single-track trail and you will come to T junction. (For a shorter ride, turn left and at the next intersection go right onto a dirt road.) Otherwise, turn right, and fork right off the main trail as you're descending. Then fork left, and left again onto a singletrack.

Continue on this trail for more than a mile, crossing several mud holes. Stay on the main trail, veering to the left. You will reach another four-way intersection. Turn left, and you will come out at another T junction on narrow dirt Sweet Sawmill Road again. Turn left on the road, and take an immediate right.

*Loop 4:* Continue on this narrow trail, turning left at another T junction. Take the next right turn and climb gently. You are now on the single-track trail that you came in on. Follow it until you rejoin the double-track trail. Then turn left onto Burnt Sawmill Road, and right to return to the parking area.

Single file on singletrack. Big River Management Area, Greenwich, Rhode Island.

# RIDE 59 COVENTRY CRUISE

This easy-to-moderate 10-mile ride uses scenic two-wheel-drive dirt roads, with some eroded areas, and several stretches on paved rural roads. This is classic New England countryside. You could be in Vermont or Maine—without the major hills. The landscape alternates between inhabited and uninhabited areas, with stands of pine trees and wetlands, small farms, open fields, and stone walls. There's also a side trip to a cranberry bog.

A rail-trail, the Trestle Trail, runs through the middle of this loop. It's rideable—but barely (at the time of this writing), because of the softer sand in many places. Still, you might want to check it out; it extends further east and west.

**General location:** At the junction of Rhodes Island Highways 102 and 117, 12 miles west of Warwick.

**Elevation change:** In a counterclockwise direction, you begin with a steady, fairly gradual climb of about 200 feet, roll gently for several miles, and descend for about 2 miles.

**Seasons:** This can be a four-season ride.

**Services:** At the trailhead, there's a general store with a deli. All other services are available to the east on RI 117 and in West Warwick, including the Bicycle Shop on RI 117 in Coventry.

**Hazards:** Be sure to give plenty of room to the occasional horse and buggy on the dirt roads (a horse farm is nearby). Watch out for motorized vehicles.

**Rescue index:** You're on traveled roads.

**Land status:** Town roads.

**Maps:** Any detailed state road map. The state has an excellent road map from the Tourism Bureau (see Appendix).

**Finding the trail:** Take Exit 10 off Interstate 95 onto RI 117 west. After 12 miles, you reach the junction with RI 102. Continue for a short distance on RI 117 and turn left onto Old Summit Road. Almost immediately, you will reach an unpaved parking area near a general store. (The partly rideable rail-trail is just beyond the store.)

**Sources of additional information:** Planning and Development, Department of Environmental Management, or Rhode Island Tourism Bureau (see Appendix).

**Notes on the trail:** Return to RI 117, turn left, and soon right onto paved Susan Bowen Road. Climb and you will reach a T junction after about a mile. Turn left, then right, then fork left almost immediately onto Sisson Road. After

A close encounter of a nineteenth-century kind. Coventry, Rhode Island.

about another mile, you reach a T junction with Cahoone Road. Turn left, and after about 2 miles, the road comes out on paved RI 117.

Turn right onto RI 117. *Caution:* Watch for faster-moving traffic on this road. After a half mile, turn left downhill onto Lewis Farm Road. (After a mile, you will pass a dirt road on the right. This road goes into secluded state land for about a mile.) After about 2 miles, Lewis Farm Road comes out onto paved Hopkins Hollow Road. Turn right, and almost immediately fork left onto a patchy asphalt road. Fork left again, and after 0.3 mile, you will reach Narrow Lane at a large rock. Turn right, and after another 0.2 mile, turn left onto Perry Hill Road, which soon becomes unpaved. (For a side trip, keep going straight on Narrow Lane. After about 1.5 miles, you will reach a large, scenic cranberry bog and a gated dirt road into a management area.) Perry Hill Road becomes paved after about 2 miles. In another mile or so, turn left at a junction with another paved road, and cruise back to the parking lot at the country store.

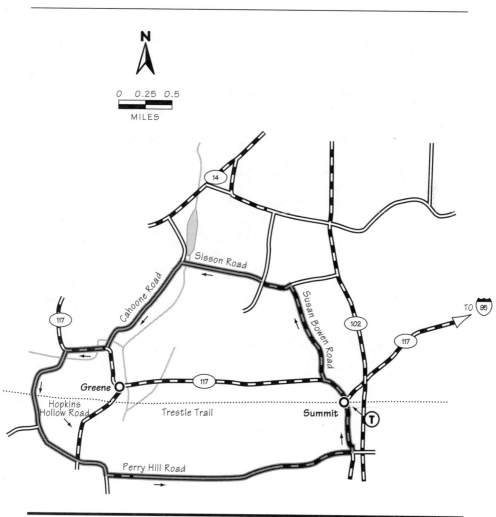

N

0 0.25 0.5
MILES

14

Sisson Road

Cahoone Road

117

Susan Bowen Road

102

TO 95

117

Greene

117

Summit

T

Hopkins
Hollow Road

Trestle Trail

Perry Hill Road

# RIDE 60 *GEORGE WASHINGTON MANAGEMENT AREA*

It's worth doing a day trip to the northwestern tip of Rhode Island to explore the rugged single-track trails and secluded dirt roads in this large state park. Riding in this well-maintained area—which connects up with more trails in Pulaski Memorial State Forest and the Buck Hill area—is a combination of easy cruising on woods roads and more tricky maneuvering on single-track trails, including parts of the 8-mile-long Walkabout Trail.

For rest and relaxation, there's also a swimming beach and picnic sites at the trailhead.

The Walkabout Trail was named after the habit of Australian tribespeople to "go walkabout" the land for days at a time—an urge not unfamiliar to outdoors-oriented people in many countries. This trail was built in 1965 by 300 Australian Navy men, who were waiting for their ship to be finished in a local shipyard. Evidently someone in charge felt that several hundred sailors needed hard work to keep them occupied. Lieutenant Unwin of their regiment wrote at the end of the trail-building undertaking: "Saturday night is barbecue night. Many of the local people and foresters come to sample our steaks. Residents of the area have been most hospitable and there will be many a lad who will be sorry to leave." How about a reunion in 2005—with maties on mountain bikes?

**General location:** Just off U.S. Highway 44, near the Connecticut border.

**Elevation change:** This terrain is rolling, with moderate climbs and descents on dirt roads, and some shorter, steeper climbs on the trails.

**Seasons:** This can be a three-season ride. As always, though, avoid riding in wet or muddy conditions. Rangers ask that cyclists avoid riding on the groomed cross-country ski trails in the winter.

**Services:** There are restrooms and a water fountain at the trailhead, and campsites available from April through October 31. All other services are along US 44.

**Hazards:** Watch for minor obstructions (like small tree stumps) on the single-track trails, an occasional vehicle or horseback rider on the dirt roads, and hikers on the trails. As always, follow the advice of equestrians when passing them, and announce your presence to hikers.

**Rescue index:** At most you will be about 2 miles from a traveled road.

**Land status:** Trails and roads on public land.

**Maps:** A map is available at the trailhead or in the headquarters (weekdays only), located on US 44, just west of the access road to the trailhead.

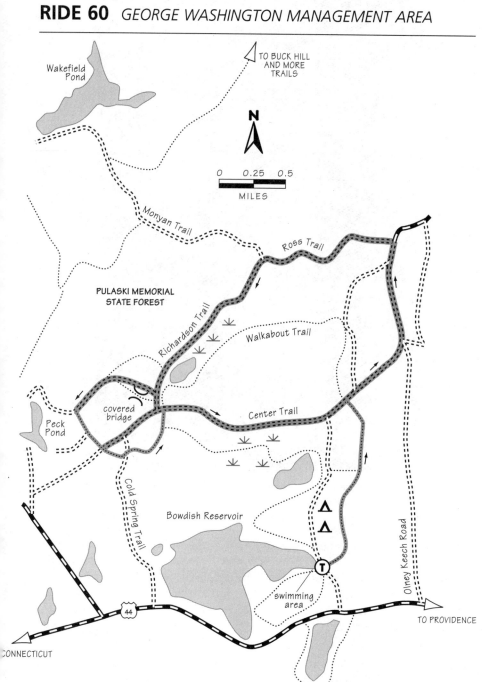

Wakefield Pond

TO BUCK HILL AND MORE TRAILS

N

0   0.25   0.5

MILES

Monyan Trail

Ross Trail

PULASKI MEMORIAL STATE FOREST

Richardson Trail

Walkabout Trail

covered bridge

Peck Pond

Center Trail

Cold Spring Trail

Bowdish Reservoir

Olney Keech Road

T

swimming area

44

TO PROVIDENCE

CONNECTICUT

Negotiating a narrow trail. George Washington Management
Area, West Gloucester, Rhode Island.

**Finding the trail:** From the east, take Exit 7 on Interstate 295, and head west
on US 44 west. After about 12.5 miles, you will pass a brown sign on the right:
"George Washington Camping Area." Turn right at this sign and drive up the
dirt road for about 0.3 mile, turning left into a gravel parking area near the
beach at Bowdish Reservoir.

From the west, take Exit 97 on I-395, and turn onto US 44 east. After about
7 miles, you will pass the access road on the left.

**Sources of additional information:** Division of Fish and Wildlife, Department
of Environmental Management (see Appendix).

**Notes on the trail:** You can do a large loop, using both the 8-mile Walkabout Trail and secluded dirt roads. As the map shows, there are many options for doing shorter rides, too.

Begin by returning to the access road and picking up the Walkabout Trail on the other side of it. This trail is well-marked with orange blazes. Also, it has 2-mile and 6-mile cutoffs marked by blue and red blazes. You will pass the blue-blazed cutoff trail on the left after about a half mile.

You come out on a dirt road (Center Trail). The Walkabout Trail becomes much more difficult on the other side, so turn right on the road. At a three-way intersection, turn left onto another dirt road. Then fork left onto the Ross Trail, another dirt road, and left again onto the Richardson Trail. (At this fork, you can also turn right for a longer ride into the Buck Hill Management Area.)

After about a mile on the Richardson Trail, you will pass a semi-hidden pond on the left and just after it on the right a gated dirt road (Inner Border Trail), which takes you to a small covered bridge.

For a shorter ride, head straight on the Richardson Trail, and soon turn left onto the Center Trail. For a longer ride, turn right onto the gated dirt road and ride across the covered bridge. Continue westward on the road, reaching Peck Pond in Pulaski Memorial State Park, which abuts this area. Then head east on either dirt roads or the orange-blazed Walkabout Trail, which intersects the road.

The last section of the Walkabout Trail becomes much wetter, so at the sign, "Cold Spring Trail," turn left on a cutoff road and pick up the Center Trail, a dirt road, to avoid several wet areas on the single-track trail. The Center Trail forks right and at a three-way intersection, it intersects the access road. Turn right and head back southward to the beach at Bowdish Reservoir.

The 1.5-mile single-track loop south of Bowdish Reservoir is rideable, but more technical. It's the purple-blazed Angell Loop Trail, running clockwise around the shore of the reservoir. After a half mile or so, the trail becomes smoother and veers to the left, away from the reservoir.

# RIDE 61 *LINCOLN WOODS STATE PARK*

This handsome park just north of Providence has about 15 miles of single- and double-track trails winding through woods, past recreational fields, and around a large lake. The area offers a fun network of trails—some flatter, smoother ones around the lake, and steep, rugged, rolling paths deeper in the woods. One out-and-back trail also leads to an overlook above the lake.

The park is also a popular swimming spot, with a beach, and it has several large playing fields (for an impromptu game of bike Frisbee or polo) as well as a 2.5-mile paved loop through the park, which is popular among road riders.

A plaque at a site along the paved loop explains that this area was actually one of the nation's first managed forests. In 1895, its creator, W. W. Baily, waxed poetic about it: "In all seasons the landscape is ravishing, but never more so than when autumn has tinted the leaves with crimson gold or claret. . . . It is not difficult to fancy oneself transferred to a locality remote from settlements, yet by climbing the hills to the north, one can see smiling villages and the evidence of thrift and civilization." Climb those hills.

**General location:** The town of Lincoln, 3.5 miles north of Providence, just off Rhode Island 146.

**Elevation change:** Although the area is relatively flat, the trails roll up and down, and the riding is sometimes made challenging by loose terrain.

**Seasons:** Good drainage makes this a possible four-season ride. As always, though, avoid riding on trails in wet conditions.

**Services:** In the summer, water, restrooms, and a concession stand are available at the beach area. All other services are found in Lincoln and Providence.

**Hazards:** Watch out for motorists (and road cyclists) on the paved road through the park; it's used as a through road. Because the park is close to several cities, it attracts many visitors; slow down on the hills and be considerate of hikers and horseback riders.

**Rescue index:** Well-traveled roads and homes surround the park.

**Land status:** State park trails.

**Maps:** There is a large, detailed map on a board on the paved road near the entrance. (From the entrance, turn left to reach it.)

**Finding the trail:** From Interstate 295, take Exit 9A onto RI 146 south toward Providence. After 3.5 miles, watch for exit signs for the park. Follow the signs, fork right at the park entrance, and you will reach a large paved parking lot on the left. From I-95 in Providence, take Exit 23 onto RI 146 north. After 4.5

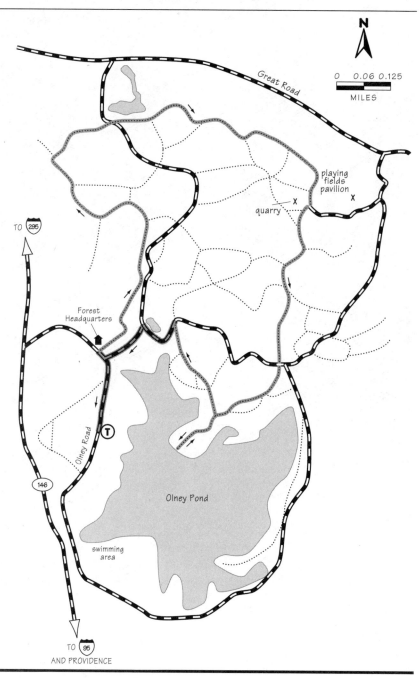

Finding a line. Lincoln Woods, Lincoln, Rhode Island.

miles, take the exit for the state park. (Note: The park charges a small fee for vehicle parking, beginning each May 1.)

**Sources of additional information:** Lincoln Woods State Park (see Appendix).

**Notes on the trail:** The paved road that loops through the middle of the park divides the area into a large outer section and a smaller inner one. Both have networks of trails, which hook up across the paved road. The inner loop is easier riding.

To begin a clockwise ride on the outer loop, fork off the paved road just left of the entrance onto a single-track trail. Follow this trail as it rolls through the woods, circumventing the park. You will cross a dead-end paved access road, pass an old stone house foundation, arrive at a playing field and pavilion on the other side of the park, and approach the lake.

Be sure to take the side trail that crosses a peninsula to reach an overlook above the lake. The lake is also used for winter riding—if it's thoroughly frozen and one has studded tires.

# Appendix: Resources

This appendix contains the key resources for the latest information about mountain biking sites in southern New England, with contacts for each of the individual rides.

First, though, it's worth noting that the Internet has become an invaluable resource for information about mountain biking areas, as well as state parks and forests, state agencies, and more. By simply typing a few keywords—say, "mountain biking" and "Massachusetts"—into a web search engine—like Alta Vista, Yahoo, or Lycos—you can find many web sites with information about mountain biking in Massachusetts, sometimes even including maps. Other possible web searches: "trails" and "Rhode Island" or the name of a state park, like, "Massasoit," or the name of a state agency, like "Connecticut" and "DEP." Try it. You'll be impressed.

The New England Mountain Bike Association (NEMBA) is the main mountain biking organization in this region. Its web site, www.nemba.org, has lots of information about local riding areas (including some maps), as well as links to many other mountain-bike groups and organizations in the region. You can contact them at: NEMBA, P.O. Box 2221, Acton, MA 01720, (800) 57-NEMBA, email: singletracks@nemba.org. If you join NEMBA, you also receive a printed newsletter.

## MASSACHUSETTS

**Department of Environmental Management (DEM)**
100 Cambridge Street
Boston, MA 02202
(617) 727-3180
(800) 831-0569 (in Massachusetts)
www.state.ma.us/dem
email: Mass.Parks@state.ma.us

**Camping Reservations**
(877) I-CAMP-MA
toll-free in Massachusetts

**Ames Nowell State Park**
Linwood Street
Abington, MA 02351
(508) 857-5850

**Arcadian Shop**
US 20/MA 7
Lenox, MA 01240
(413) 637-3010

**Beartown State Forest**
Blue Hill Road
Monterey, MA 01245
(413) 528-0904

**Bradley Palmer State Park**
Asbury Street
Topsfield, MA 01983
(978) 887-5931

Brimfield State Forest
(at Dean Pond area)
Sutcliffe Mill Road
Brimfield, MA 01010
(413) 267-9687

D.A.R. State Forest
Route 112
Goshen, MA 01096
(413) 268-7098

Douglas State Forest
107 Wallum Lake Road
Douglas, MA 01516
(508) 476-7872

Erving State Forest
Route 2
Orange, MA 01364
(508) 544-3939

F. Gilbert Hills State Forest
Mill Street
Foxboro, MA 02035
(508) 543-5850

Freetown State Forest
Slab Bridge Road
Assonet, MA 02702
(508) 644-5522

Great Brook Farm State Park
841 Lowell Street
Carlisle, MA 01741
(978) 369-6312

Harold Parker State Forest
North Turnpike Road
North Andover, MA 01845
(978) 686-3391

Holyoke Range State Park
c/o Skinner State Park
Route 116
Hadley, MA 01035
(413) 586-0350

Lenox Town Hall
Main Street
Lenox, MA 02140
(413) 637-5506

Leominster State Forest
Route 31
Princeton, MA 01541
(978) 874-2303

Lowell-Dracut-Tyngsboro State Park
c/o Lowell Heritage State Park
500 Pawtucket Boulevard
Lowell, MA 01854
(978) 453-0592

Manuel F. Correllus
(Martha's Vineyard) State Forest
P.O. Box 1612
Vineyard Haven, MA 02568
(508) 693-2540

Mashpee Conservation Office
Mashpee Town Hall
Mashpee, MA 02649
(508) 539-1414

Massasoit State Park
Middleboro Avenue
East Taunton, MA 02718
(508) 822-7405

Maudslay State Park
Curzon's Mill Road
Newburyport, MA 01950
(978) 465-7223

Mt. Greylock State Reservation
P.O. Box 138
Lanesborough, MA 01237
(413) 499-4262/4263

Myles Standish State Forest
Cranberry Road
South Carver, MA 02633
(508) 866-2526

October Mountain State Forest
Woodland Road
Lee, MA 01238
(413) 243-1778

Otter River State Forest
Route 202
Baldwinville, MA 01436
(978) 939-8962

Pepperell Selectman's Office
Town Hall
Pepperell, MA 01463
(978) 433-0333

Pittsfield State Forest
Cascade Street
Pittsfield, MA 01201
(413) 442-8992

Savoy Mountain State Forest
260 Central Shaft Road
Florida, MA 02147
(413) 663-8469

Steamship Authority
(ferry service to Martha's Vineyard)
(508) 477-8600

Stow Conservation Commission
Stow Town Building
380 Great Road (Route 117)
Stow, MA 01775
(978) 897-5078

Upton State Forest
205 Westboro Road
Upton, MA 01568
(508) 529-6923

Vineyard Offroad Bicycling
Association (VORBA)
(508) 693-4905

Windsor State Forest
River Road
Windsor, MA 01270
(413) 684-0948

Wompanoag Museum
Route 130
Mashpee, MA 02649
(508) 477-1536

Wompanoag Tribal Council
P.O. Box 1048
Mashpee, MA 02649
(508) 477-0208

Wompatuck State Park
Union Street
Hingham, MA 02043
(781) 749-7160

Wrentham State Forest
c/o F. Gilbert Hills State Forest
45 Mill Street
Foxboro, MA 02035
(508) 543-5850

## CONNECTICUT

Bureau of Outdoor Recreation
State Parks Division
Department of Environmental
Protection (DEP)
79 Elm Street,
Hartford, CT 06160
(860) 424-3200

Chatfield Hollow State Park
(contact for Wadsworth Falls
State Park)
Killingworth, CT 06419
(860) 663-2030

Connecticut Forest and Parks
Association
(860) 346-2372

Department of Environmental
Protection (DEP)
Eastern District Headquarters
(860) 295-9523

Fort Griswold State Park
(contact for Bluff Point and
Haley Farm State Parks)
57 Fort Street
Groton, CT 06340
(860) 445-1729

Groton Town Manager
45 Fort Hill Road
Groton, CT 06340
(860) 441-6630

Hometown Publications
P.O. Box 298
Trumbull, CT 06611

James L. Goodwin State Forest
Hampton, CT 06247
(860) 455-9534

Mansfield Parks and Recreation
Department
Town Hall
Storrs, CT 06268
(860) 429-3321

Mashamoquet State Park
(contact for Natchaug State Forest)
(860) 928-6121

Pachaug State Forest
P.O. Box 5
Voluntown, CT 06384
(860) 376-4075

Sleeping Giant State Park
(contact for West Rock Ridge
State Park)
200 Mt. Carmel Avenue
Hamden, CT 06518
(203) 789-7498

Westwoods Trails Committee
P.O. Box 200
Guilford, CT 06437
(860) 445-1729

## RHODE ISLAND

Arcadia Management Area
(401) 539-2356

Division of Fish and Wildlife
Department of Environmental
Management (DEM)
(401) 222-3075

Great Swamp Management Area
(401) 222-1267

Lincoln Woods State Park
2 Manchester Print Works Road
Lincoln, RI 02865
(401) 723-7892

Planning and Development
Department of Environmental
Management (DEM)
(401) 222-2776

Rhode Island Tourism Bureau
(401) 277-2601 (Rhode Island only)
(800) 556-2484

# Glossary

| | |
|---|---|
| *ATB* | All-terrain bike, a.k.a., mountain bike or fat-tired bike. |
| *ATV* | All-terrain vehicle; refers to motorized "dirt" bikes with two wheels, as well as three- and four-wheeled motorized vehicles. (A slang term for a four-wheeled off-highway vehicle is a "quad.") |
| *Bail out* | To take a shortcut back to the trailhead. |
| *Blowdowns* | Trees or large branches that have fallen across a trail, usually due to a storm. Occurs most often in the winter and appears on the trails in the spring. |
| *Blue-blazed trail* | Part of an extensive trail system throughout Connecticut, with blue markings, usually on the trees. |
| *Bunny hop* | To lift both wheels off the ground at the same time, in order to prepare for riding over an obstacle (or to impress others in a parking lot). |
| *Catch air* | To achieve the sensation of flying by launching oneself over a bump. |
| *Chain suck* | When the chain falls off the smallest chain ring—usually as you're climbing a steep hill. (It's easy to remount the chain.) |
| *Clean* | To ride through a difficult stretch of trail without having to touch a foot to the ground (see "Dab"). |
| *Clotheslined* | To be knocked off your bike by a protruding object, like a tree limb, at chest or head level. |
| *Contact station* | A small building at the entrance of a state forest or park where a ranger is stationed during the summer and fall. |
| *Dab* | To stabilize oneself by placing a foot on the ground while riding over an obstacle. |
| *DEM* | Abbreviation for Department of Environmental Management, the Massachusetts and Rhode Island state agencies that manage all state lands. |
| *DEP* | Abbreviation for Department of Environmental Protection, the Connecticut state agency that manages all state lands. |

| | |
|---|---|
| *Derailleur* | The rear part of the chain-driving mechanism that shifts the rear gears—notorious for breaking too easily if a dead branch jumps into its mechanism. |
| *Double-track trail* | A trail as wide as two bikes. |
| *Drivetrain* | The collective term for the parts of a bike involved in the movement of the chain—usually need the most cleaning and care. |
| *Drop-off* | A sudden, steep descent. |
| *Endo* | To pitch headfirst over the handlebars, a.k.a. "face plant" or "gravity check." |
| *Feather* | To squeeze the brakes lightly, in order to avoid locking them up and performing an "endo." |
| *Fire road* | A secluded, unpaved road in the woods, for fighting fires. |
| *Flexing* | Bending and relaxing one's joints to absorb bumps. |
| *Four-wheel-drive road* | A rugged, unpaved road, usually with potholes and other minor obstructions, a.k.a., jeep road. |
| *Gnarly* | Describes a trail with plenty of obstacles and/or turns and twists. |
| *Grade* | A measure of steepness, a.k.a., pitch. |
| *Greasy* | Describes a trail that is slick and dangerous. |
| *Hammer* | To ride hard. |
| *Hammered* | Exhausted, wiped out. |
| *Hammerhead* | A mountain biker who likes to ride hard and fast. |
| *Honed* | In total harmony with the trail, a.k.a., "in the zone." |
| *LBS* | Internet-speak for "local bike shop." |
| *Line* | The path on a trail with the least obstructions, as in the phrase "finding the line." |
| *Loading* | Shifting one's weight backward or forward, particularly when climbing, in order to avoid losing traction. |
| *Management area* | Term for state-owned lands in Rhode Island, usually undeveloped. |
| *Multi-use trail* | A trail intended for different kinds of users—in particular, horseback riders and motorized dirt bikes, as well as mountain bikes, hikers, and skiers. |

| | |
|---|---|
| *Out-and-back* | A ride where one doubles back on the same trail, rather than doing a loop (it's not as boring as it sounds). |
| *Punch* | To depress the front tire rapidly in preparation for lifting the front wheel over an obstacle. |
| *Rail-trail* | An ultraflat trail along a corridor that was once used by a railroad line. |
| *Rigid* | A type of mountain bike without any suspension. |
| *Scootering* | A technique for "riding" a bike when the chain has broken (it's like riding a scooter). |
| *Show-and-go* | A more casual type of group ride, in which riders are expected to arrive on time and to keep up with the leader—or go it alone. |
| *Single-track trail* | A trail just wide enough for a single bike. |
| *Slickrock* | A trail surface made up of smooth rock. |
| *Suspension* | A flexible fork, seatpost, or entire bike frame. |
| *Sweep* | One rider on some group rides who remains in the rear to make sure no one is left behind. |
| *Sweet* | Used to describe a section of trail that is highly enjoyable (a.k.a. "buff"). |
| *Switchback* | A sharp turn, usually on a steep climb, constructed to lessen the steepness. |
| *Technical* | Refers to a trail or section of trail that's more difficult to ride because of rough terrain and/or obstacles. |
| *The Berkshires* | The extreme western part of Massachusetts, known for its pastoral landscape and culture in the summer. |
| *Topo* | Short for "topographical," a type of map with contour lines on it to show elevation. |
| *Track stand* | To balance on a bike without moving forward or backward—a useful skill in mountain biking. |
| *Tuck* | To crouch to lower one's center of gravity and/or to reduce wind resistance. |
| *Turn-out* | A section of a trail widened by users to avoid a muddy spot or a large obstacle—not a recommended technique on most trails. |

| | |
|---|---|
| *Tweaked* | To be jolted laterally by a small obstacle. |
| *Two-wheel-drive road* | An unpaved road that is relatively smooth, usually because it's graded regularly. |
| *Washboarding* | Small, tight ridges on a dirt road caused by the lack of grading—they're jarring to ride over. |
| *Washed out* | A trail or section of a trail that's severely eroded, usually on a steep incline. May contain "drop-offs." |
| *Water bar* | A log or other manmade barrier placed diagonally across a trail to prevent water from running down the trail and causing erosion. |
| *Wheelie* | Lifting one wheel off the ground, usually the front wheel, to clear an obstacle, or for fun. |

# Index

Page numbers in **bold** refer to maps.
Page numbers in *italics* refer to photos.

PAUL ANGIOLILLO is a much-published freelance writer and editor. His articles have appeared in the *Boston Globe, Bicycling, Business Week, Omni, Metrosports, Dirt Rag,* and other newspapers and magazines. He is also the author of *Mountain Biking Northern New England.* Paul began "mountain" biking at the age of eight, when he rode his first bicycle into a large ditch in the woods behind his home. Later, he dodged potholes in Boston, where he served as president of the Boston Area Bicycle Coalition. Now he enjoys exploring old fire roads and trails throughout the region.

**FALCON**GUIDES® Leading the Way™

**FALCON**GUIDES® are available for where-to-go hiking, mountain biking, rock climbing, walking, scenic driving, fishing, rockhounding, paddling, birding, wildlife viewing, and camping. We also have FalconGuides on essential outdoor skills and subjects and field identification. The following titles are currently available, but this list grows every year. For a free catalog with a complete list of titles, call FALCON toll-free at 1-800-582-2665.

### MOUNTAIN BIKING GUIDES

Mountain Biking Arizona
Mountain Biking Colorado
Mountain Biking Georgia
Mountain Biking New Mexico
Mountain Biking New York
Mountain Biking Northern New England
Mountain Biking Oregon
Mountain Biking South Carolina
Mountain Biking Southern California
Mountain Biking Southern New England
Mountain Biking Utah
Mountain Biking Wisconsin
Mountain Biking Wyoming

### LOCAL CYCLING SERIES

Fat Trax Bozeman
Mountain Biking Bend
Mountain Biking Boise
Mountain Biking Chequamegon
Mountain Biking Chico
Mountain Biking Colorado Springs
Mountain Biking Denver/Boulder
Mountain Biking Durango
Mountain Biking Flagstaff and Sedona
Mountain Biking Helena
Mountain Biking Moab
Mountain Biking Utah's St. George/Cedar City Area
Mountain Biking the White Mountains (West)

■ *To order any of these books, check with your local bookseller or call FALCON* ® *at* **1-800-582-2665**.
*Visit us on the world wide web at:*
www.FalconOutdoors.com

FALCON®

# FALCON GUIDES ® Leading the Way

## FIELD GUIDES

Bitterroot: Montana State Flower
Canyon Country Wildflowers
Central Rocky Mountains
  Wildflowers
Great Lakes Berry Book
New England Berry Book
Ozark Wildflowers
Pacific Northwest Berry Book
Plants of Arizona
Rare Plants of Colorado
Rocky Mountain Berry Book
Scats & Tracks of the Pacific
  Coast States
Scats & Tracks of the
  Rocky Mountains
Southern Rocky Mountain
  Wildflowers
Tallgrass Prairie Wildflowers
Western Trees
Wildflowers of Southwestern
  Utah
Willow Bark and Rosehips

## FISHING GUIDES

Fishing Alaska
Fishing the Beartooths
Fishing Florida
Fishing Glacier National Park
Fishing Maine
Fishing Montana
Fishing Wyoming
Fishing Yellowstone
  National Park

## ROCKHOUNDING GUIDES

Rockhounding Arizona
Rockhounding California
Rockhounding Colorado
Rockhounding Montana
Rockhounding Nevada
Rockhound's Guide to New
  Mexico
Rockhounding Texas
Rockhounding Utah
Rockhounding Wyoming

## MORE GUIDEBOOKS

Backcountry Horseman's
  Guide to Washington
Camping California's
  National Forests
Exploring Canyonlands &
  Arches National Parks
Exploring Hawaii's Parklands
Exploring Mount Helena
Exploring Southern California
  Beaches
Recreation Guide to WA
  National Forests
Touring California & Nevada
  Hot Springs
Touring Colorado Hot Springs
Touring Montana & Wyoming
  Hot Springs
Trail Riding Western
  Montana
Wild Country Companion
Wilderness Directory
Wild Montana
Wild Utah

## BIRDING GUIDES

Birding Minnesota
Birding Montana
Birding Northern California
Birding Texas
Birding Utah

## PADDLING GUIDES

Floater's Guide to Colorado
Paddling Minnesota
Paddling Montana
Paddling Okefenokee
Paddling Oregon
Paddling Yellowstone & Grand
  Teton National Parks

## HOW-TO GUIDES

Avalanche Aware
Backpacking Tips
Bear Aware
Desert Hiking Tips
Hiking with Dogs
Leave No Trace
Mountain Lion Alert
Reading Weather
Route Finding
Using GPS
Wilderness First Aid
Wilderness Survival

## WALKING

Walking Colorado Springs
Walking Denver
Walking Portland
Walking St. Louis
Walking Virginia Beach

■ *To order any of these books, check with your local bookseller*
*or call FALCON ® at **1-800-582-2665**.*
*Visit us on the world wide web at:*
www.FalconOutdoors.com

FALCON®